VISI.

a pre-war childhood

for Tommy Verdijk
who turned the music
on again by accident

VISITS

Peter Robins

THIRD HOUSE (Publishers)

First published in 1992 by Third House (Publishers)
69 Regent Street, Exeter EX2 9EG, England

Typeset by Bookman Ltd, 2c Merrywood Road,
Bristol BS3 1DX

Printed and bound by Billing & Sons, Worcester

Distributed in Britain and throughout Europe by
Turnaround Distribution Co-op Ltd.,
27 Horsell Road, London N5 1XL

Cover design and photograph by Rupert Kirby

The cover painting is a detail from *Sol och ungdom*
(Youth and sun), by Jens Ferdinand Willumsen.
Reproduction is by kind permission of the
Curator of Göteborgs Konstmuseum, Sweden.

TO MY GRANDFATHER WILLIAM

would begin usually around two o'clock on a Sunday afternoon. By that time my father, mother, grandmother, brother
and I would have eaten the ritual roast beef, Yorkshire
pudding and whatever vegetables were in season. Vegetables
always included something green since cabbage and Brussel
sprouts were considered good for the blood. There were
always boiled potatoes, too, as well as baked, though they
were never counted as vegetables.

Let's choose a Sunday in May, although the month is not
crucial. I was delighted to go with my grandmother on an
outing in any weather. But let's choose May, for then there
would have been strawberries and cream for lunch. Norfolk
strawberries they would have been since there were, before
the Second World War, few importations of soft fruit from
the Mediterranean countries. The cream? Our milkman would
have left that with the weekend order. A large carton it would
have been – threepence for half a pint – brought to the door by
a horse-drawn orange and white van. Job's Dairy, unlike the
rival Express, had not yet been motorised.

My father and my grandmother invariably drank a glass of
light ale with their meal. I had a soft drink. Given any option,
I chose one of the new Corona fruit juices rather than the
more traditional Robinson's Barley Water which was held
to be good for the kidneys. My mother drank nothing. She
maintained it was not a Scottish habit to drink with one's
food. None of the rest of the family having travelled further
north than Preston, we took her word for it.

There was just time after Sunday dinner – as we called it –
for a cup of tea. Coffee was for the evening, provided there
were visitors. True, my favourite aunt served coffee not only

1

at mid-morning but after every meal. She was of a younger generation and had travelled to Biarritz, Ostend and even to the Bernese Oberland.

And then my mother would go into the kitchen to refill a kettle for the washing up. My father settled back with *The News of the World*, *The People* and *The Sunday Express*. It was time for my grandmother and I to pop into the garden to our spider-haunted lavatory before getting dressed for our trek.

Perhaps it's no more than selective memory that dims the inconveniences of childhood and preserves the pleasures, but the weather did seem kinder – or at least more predictable. On a May afternoon, I remember my grandmother being dressed in a fawn or coffee-coloured dust-coat, loosely tied at the waist, over a frock patterned either with leaves or open blossoms. She'd quite a wardrobe, being a great one for queuing on the first day of the sales as well as being able to do wonders with a remnant. Occasionally she'd buy a new hat but, more often, she would bargain for something that took her eye at one of the many bazaars that were ringed, like birthdays, on her kitchen calendar.

Whatever the weather, she'd wear a silk or chiffon scarf. When I first asked why, she whispered a reply though there was no one around to overhear.

–Because it's the neck that goes first, dear. Not that it wasn't admired when I was a girl with a bonnet and parasol, of course. Just take a look at it now though . . . no more than a bit of scrag end of mutton.

And her shoes never seemed to fit. She clomped down the stairs and along the pavements. My mother was the first person I heard using the verb. At first I thought it might be an onomatopoeic invention to suit the sound. Later, the verb became a noun and I heard references to my grandmother's old clompers. Somehow or other the Dutch klompen – clogs – had filtered into our family's vocabulary. And clomp my grandmother certainly did.

Only when childhood was nearly past did I understand that her daughters-in-law – all three of them – had long since accepted that each branch of the family was expected to supplement my grandmother's pension. One sent a pound note with the weekly letter. Another – ours – provided a midday meal throughout the week and on every other

2

Sunday; the third was counted on to keep her in shoes and stockings. When she deemed it time for a new pair of shoes, she'd wear her clompers to every family gathering as a rather noisy hint. There was no Welfare State to whom she could turn and her widow's pension was ten shillings a week; one third of the average worker's income.

So, whether in a new pair of shoes or in cracked but polished clompers, she'd set off to visit my grandfather and I'd be with her.

As an adult I've retraced that route insofar as building developments allow. It's a fair forty minutes walk. It must have taken me then, as a Junior School child, closer to an hour. Sustenance was needed for such a journey. Fortunately we'd a sweet shop and tobacconist, no more than five minutes from our house, that remained open on Sunday afternoons. Bassett's Liquorice All-Sorts was my usual choice, or maybe four ounces of fruit drops, though I disliked the pears and kept them for my unprotesting brother. My grandmother never questioned the choice, unlike my favourite aunt who'd not consult me before buying a block of Peters' Motoring Chocolate. It was plain, bitter and I loathed it but I still forgave her.

With sweets in my blazer pocket and a stout, brown carrier bag under my right arm I'd set off, hand-in-hand with my grandmother, along the Heath Road. Since there was no heathland whatsoever visible, I asked about the derivation and was told that, until the early nineteenth century, Hounslow Heath – known as the Highwayman's Paradise – had extended to the edges of Twickenham village.

Minutes later we would be walking under The Dip where I'd insist on waiting until a train, menacing as thunder, had rumbled overhead. Maybe this declivity was natural and once associated with sheep grazing on common land. More likely it had been dug by construction workers employed by the London and South Western Railway nearly a hundred years before I stood there as a child. The Dip functioned as an underpass for road traffic while the electrified track with its V trains for Kingston or Richmond, and the S for Hampton and Shepperton passed above.

Beyond us lay Twickenham Green, an open triangle of grass fringed by horse chestnuts in bloom. There the road forked

3

and, leaving some Regency villas on our left, we'd pass a motor-cycle repair shop and a Methodist Chapel. Very soon we'd see, on the Green itself, the sight-screens of cricket pitches. And then, as we drew abreast of the far, broad base of the triangle, there was First Cross Road with its terrace of small cottages, many of them covered with clapboard. These were the homes of very poor people. Not now. It has become yuppy territory. The old men who sat smoking on their Windsor chairs made in High Wycombe have long since died. So have their wives and widows who busied themselves in those small front gardens with – credit it or not – linen bonnets tied under their chins.

It was usually at about this point in our journey that my grandmother would start to recount stories from British history. She was an omnivorous reader, though none too discriminating. If she was good on deaths, like so many Victorians, she at least made them colourful. Those final moments of Nelson, Cardinal Wolsey, Edward II, Good King Charles and Thomas à Becket; I memorised the details early and could very soon anticipate the punch lines.

Whatever her predeliction for deaths in high places, my grandmother couldn't have been quite ignorant of child psychology. She must have guessed, without my voicing it, that the next ten minutes of our walk would be the boring bit.

To our left Second, Third, Fourth and Fifth Cross Roads led away towards the Hampton Road. Uninteresting in themselves, they failed totally to divert me from the sad and gory moment when Mary Queen of Scots' head fell off, dislodging her wig and revealing underneath a little grey-haired woman.

Soon came the big moment. Among hedgerows bordering the pavements to our right there was, almost unexpected' a rusty iron gate. I'd be watching for it, even as I listened a... chewed those bitter hedgerow sprigs that my grandmother called poor man's bread and cheese. Once at this old kissing gate, we'd leave the dusty Staines Road with its occasional motor-bike and sidecar or even more occasional Number 90 bus making for Hanworth and Sunbury.

Beyond the hedges a field stretched away in front of us before dropping down to the muddy little River Crane. We'd keep to a narrow path that was bounded, on our left, by three thick

4

wires strung between irregular wooden posts. This, rather insecurely, fenced off a private estate.

Once we'd found a suitable gap in the fencing, I'd open the carrier bag while my grandmother called an aged threadbare donkey. I'd extend to it – very cautiously – the outer leaves of the cauliflower or cabbage we'd eaten an hour earlier. It was always a nerve-wracking moment, for the donkey's teeth appeared huge and yellow to me: as terrifying as anything in a nightmare.

Yet I must have developed some trust in the animal soon enough for I gave it merely half my attention. I'd be scanning the broad and well-tended lawns that spread beyond the donkey's paddock. Would he appear? He did not always do so.

The poor man, so I've learned since, was dying of cancer. Most afternoons, though, from April to October, he'd amble very slowly into view and lift a hand to wave. A wave – especially for us – from a real live king. A quasi-rural manor house, set in what we locals called King Manuel's Estate, was the retreat of the exiled king of Portugal.

With luck I'm recollecting accurately, rather than filtering memory through photographs I've glanced at subsequently, but I recall him as not particularly tall – for a king! Whatever the weather he wore a Homburg hat and, very often, a top coat and muffler. Colours? Well, he was distant then, physically. Time has now pushed him further out of focus so all I can offer is an impression of grey and beige.

I'm sure my grandmother never curtsied, despite her interests in history and in royals. I certainly didn't bow, though I always lifted my navy-blue school cap to wave back.

Having fed the King's donkey, we'd wander on through that field scented with clover and baked grass until, somehow, we crossed the River Crane. Was there a rickety wooden bridge or did we tread warily across a couple of old planks? Whatever it may have been, we were soon on the further grassy slope that led up and out into Powder Mill Lane. A quiet road then but one important to me for I knew that we'd no more than another five minutes' trudge to our destination.

Freshly cut flowers were always on sale at a couple of stalls set out on either side of the cemetery gates. The vendors bought locally or, just as often, had grown them on one of the many allotments that bordered a new arterial road cutting through from Richmond to Hanworth: the Great Chertsey Road that extended nowhere near as far as Chertsey. We bought whatever flowers were in season. I say we because I would have been given a shilling by my father.

We'd not make directly for my grandfather's grave. First, to the porch of a small chapel in which funeral services were held. Outside, set in the ragstone walls, were iron hooks supporting half a dozen watering-cans and, below them, a tap on a standpipe. By the time I was seven, I could help my grandmother carry a filled can between us. Another couple of years and I could stagger with it alone, without soaking my clothes or the gravel path.

Making our way along narrow strips of grass between fresh slabs of marble and other, untended mounds on which couch grass and dandelions flourished, we'd reach the grave of William Robins 1869–1933. A frame of white marble retained a flower bed, in the middle of which there was an unfussy urn. Through the perforated zinc cover of that we could stick our stems of sweet william or some bold chrysanthemums to replace those dahlias, or maybe garnet roses, that had wilted in the sun.

Before tackling all that, my grandmother would have reached down among the edging plants to retrieve a small trowel she kept hidden there. With this, and with the help of a pair of blunt scissors she carried in her handbag, the weekly ritual of weeding and trimming could begin.

She worked calmly and methodically, just as she did when cleaning the glass on my grandfather's portrait that stood on her dressing-table. I'd sit on the corner of a nearby grave and study the more dreadful excesses of nineteenth-century sentiment that surrounded me. The words – quotations on slabs and urns and crosses – remain more vivid to me than the sculptural extravagances on which they'd been engraved. Row upon row of people who 'fell asleep.' Phrases from the more lachrymose ballads still sung in my relatives' homes on Sunday evenings: 'I hear you calling me...' ... 'Until' ... 'Down the Vale'.

This landscape, with its configurations of loss, did not terrify me. What else was it but an affirmation of the conversations of those adults who surrounded me? Even my own grandmother who – to me – symbolised laughter and vivacity, would add a

6

proviso whenever she was invited to a picnic or a party: 'If the Great Reaper sees fit to spare me.'

My childhood was one in which contemporary cousins – and their cousins – appeared only sporadically. For the most part I was alone among sedate middle-aged and elderly relatives – with the single exception of my favourite aunt and uncle. Only recently married, they spoke of cocktail parties, Mediterranean beaches and West End Theatres. These tantalising references shimmered in my imagination like sunlight on the Thames in June. This lively young couple became – though I did not rationalise it – my only tangible evidence of anything worthwhile in the way of existence between leaving school and joining those innumerable relatives whose conversations reverted constantly to reflections on the day before yesterday. Whenever my white or grey-haired elders did speak of the present it was, more often than not, in muted tones liberally punctuated with sighs. Having puckered their lips and nodded their heads, they'd make references to some unfortunate absentee from the supper table who'd 'got it,' and whose life could now be measured in 'weeks rather than months.' Cancer, strokes and angina became an almost inescapable prospect and all my school work little more than a preparation for that long sleep in the watery gravel of the Thames Valley.

While my grandmother wrapped the latest crop of weeds in a sheet of newspaper, I'd try to recall what I could remember of the man whose remains were six feet below us. I knew the exact measurements. My grandmother had told me:

–Six feet leaves enough room for me, my dear. I won't keep him waiting long.

Such images as I did recollect never included my grandparents as a couple.

I recalled a room over Twickenham Post Office in the London Road. Windows larger than those in our house or in the sitting rooms of any other relative or neighbour. An upright shadow, no more, seated in a Victorian wing-back chair facing both the fire and me. Between where I stood, not far from the door and those great windows overlooking the shops, an oak dining-table covered with chenille. The number of times I banged my shins on the carved intricacies of those table legs is beyond count. It was a table styled as though designed by William Morris. Whether my grandparents bought it as new I don't know. How they afforded it is certain: with the Christmas tips my grandfather received in 1889.

Having started work as a telegraph boy in Portsmouth, he graduated speedily to postman. Only twenty years old, William Robins secured for himself one of the most envied walks in the city: the affluent suburb of Southsea. He needed it. He and my grandmother married hastily in the autumn of 1888. There'd been a Bank Holiday romp in August on the Isle of Wight and Lavinia was pregnant.

William's Christmas tips as a postman bought – during the following years – not only that dining-table and some unusually plain but pleasing chairs. There was also a grandfather clock – we did not call it a long-case. This, too, stood in that sitting room over the London Road post office.

What other image do I honestly recollect of that Twickenham Post Master who died from encephalitis when I was a toddler? One more: an even less substantial shadow.

A white face against white bed-linen, propped up in a brass bedstead set obliquely against a corner of the room so that the foot appeared to extend half-way towards us. I stood there, again in a doorway, holding my mother's hand, on a midwinter's afternoon. Of any conversation that might have taken place I remember nothing. But, on the stairs once more and making for the street, my mother's tart remark still echoes:

–The very idea of leaving a dying man to go raking round the shops for bargains. It's disgraceful. They should be downright ashamed of themselves.

From someone, maybe my grandmother or perhaps an aunt, she'd heard that, were my grandfather to recover, there'd be some brain damage that would result in a distortion of the personality. This might well cause him, it was supposed, to wander round exposing himself in public. My mother's response was terse and, to the rest of the family, shocking:

–Then I hope the poor fellow dies.

And he did, though I was kept in ignorance of the funeral.

My grandmother's weeding of the grave completed for another week, I'd be called to empty whatever brackish water remained in the flower urn onto the nearest path. I can still smell the sour and sickly odour produced by those slightly glutinous stems. The fresh bunches trimmed, my grandmother would grind the ends of the stalks with the heel of her shoe to ensure that the blooms would last for the better part of the following seven days.

We'd then step back a pace. It was rather the movement one might make on a formal and public occasion – a parade, say, or when being presented to royalty. Then we'd stand in silence a moment looking at the Middlesex soil that covered my grandfather. It's possible my grandmother was saying a prayer. She may have been reminiscing. I was doing neither but I'd sufficient experience as a choirboy to assume a solemn face. Not a word was said until we'd collected the empty watering-can and were on our way back to the chapel porch. As we reached the corner beyond which we'd no longer be able to see our flowers stirring in a light breeze, my grandmother would turn and say:

–I'll be back next Sunday, old stick . . . if not sooner.

The awful overtones of that final phrase impressed themselves on me more than any weeping or noisy blowing of the nose could have done.

There was no one I knew among the steady trickle of the living that made its way along the gravel paths as we were leaving. None of the few children was from my school. My grandmother, however, was a gregarious soul. Didn't she chat with easy affability to strangers in our station yard whenever there were charity day collections? As she pinned linen or paper flowers on suits and topcoats she could make endless small talk with people whose names she never knew. It was this knack – quite foreign to me, for I'd been dared to speak to strangers –that I put to use years later as a radio reporter. When first sent into the crowded rush-hour streets to sound out commuters on some topic of interest I was terrified. My only comfort, while engaged in this exercise known in the trade as vox pops, was that if an old lady of sixty-five could manage it, so could I.

There seemed to be no end to the shuffling line of black-swathed crones to whom my grandmother would chat as we left the cemetery. Although Queen Victoria had long since died, elderly widows remembered her and wore their mourning weeds with a streamer of net drifting from a peaked bonnet to well below their waists.

9

The Widow of Windsor had been their pattern in more than clothing. They seemed almost to relish the role that bereavement had thrust upon them. If there was sadness and stoicism – and I'm sure there was – then I'm equally certain that they'd muted pleasure in being the focus of sighs and commiseration.

I cannot truthfully state that I recall my grandmother being similarly garbed but I do have some recollection of a discussion between her, my mother and my youngest aunt. The exact date on which she could appear in public with a suggestion of purple or grey in her outfit appeared to be important. Too early a hint of frivolity would elicit a sniffy comment from the neighbours.

At last we'd passed the flower sellers again and were on our way home. It was then, when I knew that thoughts about my grandfather would be uppermost in her mind, that I'd ask my grandmother more about him.

A practical man he seems to have been and not without artistic interests. A man who had sat up throughout one Christmas Eve dismantling that same grandfather clock he'd bought very cheaply because it would not function. By the time my grandmother had come down on Christmas morning to make tea, the clock had been reassembled and was working as well as it has ever done this past century.

William was a self-taught musician who, in his twenties, had formed a pop group of mandolin players to entertain not just his fellow postal workers at staff parties and summer outings. There were also gigs at working men's clubs and harvest suppers in the chapels and churches across Greater Portsmouth. Twenty years ago I met an elderly relative of my grandfather who'd accompanied the group at the piano. Though she couldn't call to mind any particular numbers they'd played, she was sure they'd included popular tunes of the day lifted from the early musical comedies.

My grandfather remained a postman for only a few years. Soon he was promoted to supervise a new generation of telegraph boys in the office where he himself had begun. Portsmouth, smaller then, was a city in which, by chance, my mother's mother was working as cook for the staff canteen at the main post office. It's to her that I'm indebted for a glimpse of Grandfather William at work. A right little martinet he appears to have been. A stickler for appearances, it seems, who was held in some awe by those teenage messenger boys. He called them to a quasi-military parade and inspection every morning. Haircuts were checked and there was more than a glance at the back of youthful necks for evidence of any tide mark. A dozen pairs of hands had to be extended to show pared and clean finger-nails. There's little doubt that William's own upbringing as the only child of a Royal Marine set a pattern and a standard for him that he imposed, unquestioningly, on others.

The outbreak of the 1914-1918 war brought him further promotion: to Inspector of Posts in Winchester. With his three sons now young adults: two married and two of the three away at the Western Front, William had time to develop his musical talent in another direction. He learned to play the violin competently.

Later, in the peace following Versailles, he became a Methodist lay preacher, cycling out to the Hampshire villages on Sunday evenings. At work, his final promotion to Twickenham would not have daunted him. What is today little more than another London suburb had, sixty years ago, more rural touches than I have suggested. And William was no stranger to the capital. Even before the 1914-1918 war he and my grandmother had cycled from their pleasant house in Laburnum Grove, Southsea, up over Portsdown Hill and north, through Petersfield, towards the Hog's Back. At the end of a long day they'd reach the homes of William's distant relatives who'd settled in London's newer, sprawling suburbs.

An only child himself, my grandfather had many cousins. His father, another William, had been the eighth of a brood of ten reared in Black Pit Cottage on the outskirts of Tedburn St Mary in Mid-Devon. And *his* father, John Robins, although just another poorly paid farm labourer by 1829, had come of prosperous farming stock.

It was during the decade that followed the Napoleonic wars that Robbyn's Hey, first recorded as a farm in Henry III's reign, had been sold. Like other farmers on those gentle hillsides that rose to Dartmoor on the west and sloped eastwards to the River Creedy, the Robins family had done well through supplying grain and meat to Wellington's army and

Nelson's navy. With the peace of 1815 came cheaper imports from defeated France. The war profiteers were bankrupted and sold up. The newly impoverished families dispersed and my own great-grandfather, all thoughts of education abandoned became, for a few years, a child who scared crows for a penny a week in fields that his father once owned.

In 1842, the rapidly extending web of railway lines reached Exeter. Within a decade of that event, there'd been an almost complete scattering of my own family. The crow-scaring child, by then a fresh-complexioned lad with brown hair and blue eyes, enlisted for the Royal Marines at Topsham Barracks. His many brothers and sisters – with a couple of exceptions – had left for London or for what they would have called the colonies of Australia and New Zealand. So it was to visit their children: cousins who had made good in Croydon, others who'd fared not so well in Holland Park, that my grandparents set off along the road to London in the early years of this century. En route they fortified themselves with an occasional glass of Burton ale and a pile of home made pasties.

Once, towards the end of his life, Grandfather William was taken by his own children in a splendid Singer touring car with a dicky seat back to mid-Devon in search of any surviving relatives. For a whole day – or so my grandmother told me – they combed Exeter in search of the Packhorse Inn. It was maintained by family gossip that it had been owned by my grandfather's uncle Jim. Oral family history is generally reliable for a span of three generations. It was in this instance. What my questing relatives did not know was that there were –until after the 1914-1918 war – two pubs of the same name in the city. It didn't really matter that they concentrated on the wrong Packhorse. James Robins, cow-keeper and publican, had died in 1911 and his property disappeared in a modernisation scheme within ten years.

Almost all of this I gleaned from my grandmother as we recrossed the River Crane and headed once more for King Manuel's Estate. We'd make a second stop by the field near the donkey. There we'd refill the brown paper carrier; this time with dandelions or cowslips for a fresh brew of my grandmother's home-made wine. With a final wave to the King who, provided a late afternoon breeze had not got up, would be drinking tea or coffee on the verandah, we'd make for home.

I inherited only two souvenirs of William Robins. There was his gold pencil – but that disappeared when my house was done over some years ago. I do still have, however, a studio portrait of him, posed formally in some photographer's neo-Gothic chair. The spats over his shoes and the winged collar preserve him in a world that had passed already when I was a child. The set of his mouth, though, and his slightly ironic glance are familiar enough to me in my shaving mirror.

As to what he might have been like as a parent, I feel I've more than a hazy notion. My own father was his eldest child. Parents inevitably practise on their first-born, either by reinforcing those traditions in which they themselves have been reared or by being radically progressive. Even that second option has been open to ordinary folk only for the past two or three decades. It certainly didn't exist for a postman in the closing years of Victoria's reign.

My father's approach to me, in his turn, was probably a direct reflection of William's treatment of *him*: distant, inhibited from displays of affection through terror of seeming unmanly, obsessed with cleanliness and order, frightened of alienating those with some petty authority, and too much gratitude for the smallest kindness.

And yet . . . and yet, William seems to have broken free of such constraints over the years in a way that my own father never did. Was it career success alone? I think not. There's small doubt in my mind that much of his liberation can be attributed to his hasty but never regretted marriage. In short, to the affection of my fun-loving, saucy and slightly malicious grandmother.

TO THE ROBINSONS

were complex operations. Adventures to me but, to my parents, wearing on the nerves.

Not that Uncle William and Aunt Renée ever lived, during my childhood, even one quarter of the distance that separated us from our relatives in Portsmouth or Leicester. The Robinsons' increasingly impressive houses, however, were set in residual villages on the grassier fringes of Outer London. Visits to them involved a cross-suburban trek.

We had, in a literal sense, to keep up with the Robinsons as Uncle William progressed through these villages, first with a hod and cement bucket, later with wage packets and an employer's eye. No sooner had a tube line been extended into the countryside or a pot-holed road made up to accommodate motorised traffic than he was on the spot, acquiring land on which to construct avenue upon avenue of the nicer type of semi-detached villa.

We visited my mother's elder brother and his family on those intervening Sundays when my grandmother wasn't lunching with us. The lingering impression of those journeys is not one of sunny mornings. I recollect long waits on foggy railway platforms such as Raynes Park, or at damp bus stops in drowsy little towns like Ashtead or Leatherhead. These were the years before Uncle William peaked. By 1937 he was able to send his car to pick us up.

It was not only the protracted journeys, made more so by the vagaries of the public transport system, that frayed my parents' nerves. There was always the certainty that the master builder would be waiting in his porch, gold turnip-watch in hand, checking our arrival time. There was a standard arrangement that we should present ourselves by twelve thirty for a one o'clock meal. My mother would say airily that she didn't care tuppence for the frown of her brother's displeasure since we were not his workmen who were expected to report on site not one second later than seven thirty in the morning.

More privately, I'm certain that she was very ready to play on the realisation that she was William's favourite sister. If he was a bit of a bully – and I began to suspect that when I was very young – then so could she be. They respected one another and, after a ritual of tut-tuttings because we were late, any initial coolness was forgotten.

Ickenham, in North-West Middlesex, is the first place with which I associate this overbearing uncle and his nail-biting wife. I've a very clear image of myself standing by Aunt Renée near a tea-table in a butter-coloured room. An impression of space beyond an open window remains with me: of birds singing and of country smells. Perhaps Uncle William was with his two or three employees, checking the footings for some new row of villas. At first, he could afford to hire no more than a couple of jobbers. The team of craftsmen, the personal architect and his own detached house came at the end of the decade, together with the maid, a woman to help with the rough work, and a gardener.

Did he already dream, in Ickenham, of a future that included such symbols of prestige, as well as of a leisure that would encompass theatrical first nights, regular lunches with the local member of parliament and receptions at palaces? I think now that he very probably did.

It had been impressed on me, before I was able fully to comprehend what was being said, that my uncle was a Living Miracle. This opinion had been voiced originally by some member of staff at the Royal Free Hospital after William Charles Thorpe Robinson had been operated on when he was five years old. For some reason that I never did discover, he'd had a lung removed. The remaining organ served him well enough for a further seventy-five years.

I know nothing of his schooling other than that it would have been in Inner South London and that he left when he was twelve years old. His father – a grandfather unknown to me – had been a Metropolitan Police detective turned wine importer who worked in those faintly Dickensian vaults that

15

still exist under the arches supporting Waterloo Station. The man died suddenly when William was eight and the Robinson family, impoverished, moved to a couple of rooms in one of the Guinness's Buildings along the Walworth Road. No apprenticeship could be afforded, despite some help to the family from Masonic funds. The next vignette of young William – provided for me by family chatter – is of a teenager holding horses' heads along the Thames Embankment. Listening to this, I wondered at first whether these might have been circus animals waiting to perform in a Big Top that had long since been removed from the riverside gardens. Or were they, perhaps, runaway drays such as those illustrated in the improving tales that elderly relatives thrust at me on wet afternoons? I was wrong, but the images I constructed for myself were colourful and disturbing. Like King Manuel's donkey, large horses were menacing. I cared only for the small and more docile creatures I encountered in our well-ordered suburb.

Having probed a little, I discovered that the horses' heads in question were attached to bodies and they, in turn, were harnessed to the carriages of the wealthy. Echoes of late Victorian London began to sound for me: horses pawing the cobbles by tram lines under the plane trees; Uncle William sheltering from the drizzle but still gripping the tinkling reins; drivers stamping frosty pavements outside theatres and restaurants along the Strand; slivers of laughter at last as crowds spilled out from the theatre foyers and hotel vestibules.

One lung my uncle might have had but there was resilience in the lad. Pea-soup fogs and damp mists rising from the recently embanked Thames did not affect him. But something did permeate the callow teenager: the experience itself. It moulded him: cast him early as a classic instance of the self-made businessman. By the light of those gas lamps along the river he glimpsed a life very different from the rough and tumble under paraffin flares at the stalls by the Elephant and Castle; one much easier than queuing for bargains and damaged goods as the shops in East Lane market closed. As he became aware of a more opulent world he wanted it for himself and his family – in that order.

Lacking an apprenticeship, he'd no means of entering this bourgeois paradise other than by hiring himself and his

16

hands. By day he became a builder's labourer, studying the carpenters, tilers, plumbers and painters at their work. By night he studied those who'd made it into the good life.

He was twenty-three when World War I began. He tried – despite the missing lung – to enlist. He was rejected. By 1917, however, medical examinations had become cursory. More fodder was needed after the carnage of the Western Front and the endless losses at sea. William Robinson, Able-Bodied Seaman, was soon on his way to Archangel.

He would tell me, on visits later than that first one to Ickenham, of quayside scenes at that Arctic port in the immediate aftermath of the Soviet Revolution. His descriptions matched his views: simple, forthright and colourful. At the foot of the ship's gangway, he recalled seeing clusters of weeping aristocrats. They were described invariably as princesses and archduchesses. They may have been. They certainly were to young William. In return for an illegal passage out of the newly established Soviet state, these women would extend to the sailors a mound of jewels cupped in their hands.

My uncle remembered mostly their beauty and their wealth. Both must have contrasted vividly with the destitution – and the malformation of limbs and minds that that stemmed from it – which had surrounded him in the tenements and corner shops along the Walworth Road.

Yet, even among the pawn shops and stinking detritus of those mean streets, he found one beautiful young woman who did not, when she spoke, sound like the flower girl Eliza Doolittle. Aunt Renée, the daughter of a local newsagent, had been born in Sussex. Whatever my uncle later criticised as defects, Renée was kind, uncomplicated and endowed with common sense. How far he shared with her, before their marriage, his dream of affluence, I don't know. She may have listened and smiled and supposed that it would fade, as it usually does, in the daily struggle for bread. That it did not do so was one factor contributing to their sour and miserable marriage. Renée's own dream was simple: a clean and pleasant home away from the rancid urban landscape in which they'd met. She'd no interest in the superficial glitter of social life or the chatter of those she referred to as lounge lizards.

In addition to coping with his hunger for social mobility, Aunt

Renée had to contend with her husband's bullying. Easy to say that she should have learned to bully back. He had the advantage for he could practise daily on his workmen. She had only her children on whom she might have perfected any technique and that she refused to do.

She concentrated on rearing their three boys and one surviving girl. He – perceiving that there was more to the decade than the Jarrow Hunger March and the obscene unemployment in South Wales – moved swiftly from one Outer London village to the next, translating the fantasies of the new middle class into pseudo-Tudor residences. As he did so, he envisaged privately some edifice even more gracious for himself.

Yet what he constructed for others was good. He'd a sneering contempt for what he termed dismissively 'jerry-built terraces.' No doubt he had in mind those endless rows of workers' dwellings thrown up, during his youth, around the docklands of East and South London. So his villas, with cleaner air between them and as many trees as possible preserved, rose course by course among the fields and market gardens of West Middlesex and North-East Surrey. Parades of shops – usually including a Dewhurst the butcher and a Halfords for cycles – followed. Soon there were new bus stops and sometimes an extra railway station.

I remember clearly walking with my mother between concrete mixers along a not quite completely made-up road late one Boxing Day afternoon. Precast standards for the street lighting were in place though the lamps were not yet operating. We stepped warily around the freezing puddles on our way to a reunion of my mother's family. For us, Christmas Day was always spent with my grandmother and my father's folk. On Boxing Day, all the daughters-in-law were at liberty to visit their own kin. So we trudged from Ewell West Station to the only full gathering of the Robinsons that I can recall.

Some of them remain no more than silhouettes with names but Aunt Renée was certainly at the fireside, nursing my newest cousin. Around her, on a carpet littered with gift-wrappings, were her older children as well as my more remote cousins from Preston: contemporaries but with strange accents, sandy hair and freckles. They had inherited a characteristic colouring from our common ancestors in the Scottish Highlands. I had not.

18

Memories of arriving at Uncle William's when he had really made it are far more distinct. My eldest cousin, John, was by then working as his father's chauffeur. If not driven all the way from home, we'd be met at Ashtead Station and taken in the Bentley to the last double-fronted villa in a cul de sac: Old Pastures, Chaffer's Mead.

In the huge sitting room there was a grand piano which no one, other than my toddling brother and my father, could play. From this room, French doors led onto a patio and then to half an acre of garden. Across the entrance hall – as extensive as the ground floor of our own house – there was the unheard-of luxury of a downstairs cloakroom as well as a chilly but imposing dining room. The kitchen? Well, that was twice the size of any I'd ever seen.

Prosperity had brought William to Chaffer's Mead but Renée had opted out. She liked us, so it was not as a favour that she shared the dining table and was waited on by the maid. Usually – when my uncle had invited guests – she ate in the kitchen with the staff. William swore it was to embarrass him; Renée contended it was not. She'd no objection to her husband playing the fine gentleman, as she put it, and having sherry parties with his friends. She'd just no interest in such gatherings and would take no part in them.

The grand friends' era had certainly begun for William Robinson. The route to it had been through charity donations. One benefit evening led to further invitations. The former holder of horses' heads drew closer to crowned heads, heads yet to be crowned and heads unadorned by anything other than increasingly tarnished tiaras. There was also an unending queue of knights' widows eager for a free cup of tea at the Dorchester or the Hyde Park Hotel. And William was flattered to settle the bill. There was a tide of harpies, too, ready to provide an open bedroom door in return for a champagne supper and a seat in the stalls. William, by then in his fifties, was not merely affluent. He could be genial, too, and impressive in his tail suit and diamond studs.

Aunt Renée guessed but did not care. She was content to remain at home with her children and a novel. Once, permed and lacquered in Mayfair, swathed in gold lamé and with long gloves to hide those broken nails and their bleeding quicks, she did allow herself to be pushed forward at a St James's

Palace tea party to present a purse of sovereigns to one of the royals. It was some benefit organised by a charity for children and Renée felt one might trust a royal to see that the money made its way beyond the committee's expense accounts.

That one afternoon excepted, William would have faced the great, the good and the gaudy alone or with what my mother termed an adventuress on his arm, had it not been for my parents. They had lived in India as the sun was going down on the long day of the Raj. They knew a dessert knife from a fingerbowl. So it was no desire on William's part to patronise them that led him to include my parents in his party on those ever more frequent occasions when he was involved in some West End jamboree. He liked my mother and father and his honesty in business dealings extended to an honesty in self-estimation. He knew he was weak on the minutiae of etiquette. My mother, by contrast, might have listed on a curriculum vitae seven years' experience of the subtle snobberies of colonial life, not to mention her weekly perusal – in one of the women's magazines – of tips by Una, Lady Trowbridge. My mother was good on the bowing though she was never a scraper.

As a child I'd watch the chauffeured car crunch slowly along the gravel of Laurel Avenue to collect my parents for the first night of a musical or the gala performance of an opera. My father genuinely enjoyed the music; he was possibly the only one of the quartet who did.

Next morning I'd enjoy a small netted bag of home-made chocolates or some other delicacy that my mother had secreted in her purse for me. As I munched them I'd hear details of the performance: not so much about the one on stage, more about the intervals when the untitled studied the titled and the titled evaluated industrial peerages against old money.

Even those moments before the curtain rose on the first act could be more fascinating for onlookers than the abilities of any diva. A regular chorus of lingerers would be scattered around the foyer. They'd be toying with their programmes and waiting – though pretending not to – for the arrival of some guest of honour. I was told, with a sigh, of one royal duchess for whom the photographers of a kinder generation would pause, hoping that she'd overcome a spasm of facial tics so that they might snap her, smiling, for the morning papers. My mother would sigh again.

–That dreadful drunkard of a husband, of course.

Since the royal lady had arrived unaccompanied by anyone other than her lady-in-waiting, I was at a loss to understand how her husband could be responsible for her nervous condition.

–When you're older, dear, you'll understand.

Years later I did hear folk-tales about this particular duke's behaviour when drunk. He was reported to have fallen flat on the Australian tarmac in front of a welcoming guard of honour. More to the point, when his wife was around he became insistently lecherous.

My mother's accounts of such evenings would always end with the journey home, well after midnight. The basic route never varied, even though it might involve a detour. Under the plane trees – older now – and along a street where the tramlines still ran: the Thames Embankment. She would smile a little as she described the lights between the trees, the coffee stalls and the homeless sheltering from the drizzle. She left me to make the connection and, very soon, I did so.

In general, William Robinson moved faultlessly onwards and upwards across the red carpets. Only one dreadful gaffe was ever related to me. Even that need not have cost him the knighthood he'd been promised by 1939.

Having acquired a couple of tickets for a charity dinner that was to provide relief for a leper colony, he bribed a waiter to reserve seats at a table facing King George VI. The coffee served, a toastmaster acted as the nicer type of auctioneer. He turned to the top table. The king indicated that he would be prepared to maintain two poor sufferers in Africa in some kind of lifestyle. The toastmaster bowed and turned to face the other tables. Uncle William raised his hand instantly:

–I'll support three.

The silence, my mother reported, was frightening. He should have taken her with him instead of an actress who was resting. My mother was more prudent when royalty was around, even though she could be critical of them. Returning from a ball some months after the leper faux pas, she told my brother and me that she'd danced with Uncle William very near an extra special person.

–Who? Who?

–O, she was an insignificant little creature in need of a decent hair wash and set.

At last she told us. We were both aghast that she could be referring to the future Queen of England.

Chances of William's knighthood evaporated with the outbreak of the 1939-1945 war, though he may not have realised it immediately. Having peaked, he began unwittingly a descent on a parabolic curve from which there's seldom a recovery. He'd just bought a park: Ashtead Park to be exact. A cheque for half a million pounds had been signed on the false assumption that another piece of paper, signed in Munich, would ensure a continuance of the cloudless prosperity that my uncle was beginning to enjoy.

Within months, the government had imposed restrictions on domestic building. William's work force had been conscripted or deployed on war work. Years of idleness followed for my uncle, punctuated only by daily forays through the Surrey market towns in search of under-the-counter delicacies paid for with currency notes rather than ration coupons. Ashtead Park was included in the Green Belt Plan for post-war Greater London. It was bought finally on a compulsory purchase order by Surrey County Council for – in real terms – far less than Uncle William had paid for it.

In those tranquil Sunday afternoons before Munich none of us guessed that Chaffer's Mead, with its winding staircase of English oak, would ever have to be sold. Politics were seldom discussed. At most, there'd be an exchange of commonplaces between my father and my uncle, both benevolent Conservatives. The stained-glass mediaeval knight in a window on the landing could be expected to guard William Robinson, his investments and his family for decades to come.

His opulence and humourless displeasure aside, I associate this uncle – more than any other relative – with food. It was sometimes difficult to decide whether my younger brother's nausea on our return journeys from the Robinsons should be attributed to the motion of trains and buses, or to that surfeit of luxuries with which we'd all been crammed from arrival to departure.

Work and food were his twin passions. He talked constantly of both. I see him now, moving impatiently on his chair or standing restlessly in a doorway if anyone attempted to discuss anything else.

He was, until the last few years of his life, a teetotaller. We, however, on arrival would be plied with sherry or soft drinks and endless trays of tea. Lunch was gargantuan: a baron of beef from Kingston Market or the most obese turkey or goose that the Mac Fisheries in Richmond could supply. With this came as many vegetables as one would need to call to mind in solving the most difficult crossword. Huge summer puddings followed, or great bowls of fruit, slopping over fairly tasteful crockery scarcely out of the Lawleys of Regent Street wrappers. There was no washing machine. There was, instead, a woman from the village who'd be calling the following day for our stained Irish linen napkins and the soiled tableclothes.

In fine weather we'd try to work off our post-prandial lethargy by playing croquet on the lawn. In winter we'd walk the frosty lanes. Whatever the season, there'd be a mid-afternoon tour of the latest half-completed avenue in which the houses were already spoken for. We admired:

–Central heating? Incredible . . . no more spluttering gey- sers. . . Pine? . . . All the way from Sweden? How amazing . . . And all the fruit trees have been preserved in the garden? . . . That's really good planning.

We said much the same on every tour. It was expected and the compliments were accepted with a genial smile. I don't recall Aunt Renée accompanying us once.

She'd be preparing tea while the maid coped with the washing-up from lunch. By four thirty we'd be in the dining room again, toying with a lobster salad. My uncle would have dismembered a couple of the creatures. Each time the maid's back was turned he'd palm hunks of flesh into his mouth, adept as any fairground conjuror. After the salad there'd be trifle with clotted cream as deep as your thumb, followed by éclairs and mille feuilles bought on William's Friday afternoon trips to Harrods or Fortnum and Mason.

Distended with food and bemused by my uncle's accounts of interminable wrangles with suppliers and solicitors, we'd prepare to leave at around seven in the evening after a final tray of tea and petit fours.

William referred habitually to my mother as his 'poor sister.'

It was a role at which she laughed. Yet it was one that she was happy to play as she culled whatever was on offer. As we left, she'd be loaded with tins of food, the carcass of a fowl or lobster, and an almost unmanageable bunch of flowers torn from the earth to the despair – no doubt – of the gardener the following morning.

Chaffer's Mead was not a house in which I would have wished to be reared. Playing to us as his public, William Robinson embodied both the lavishness and the sentimentality of a Dickensian benefactor. He'd some experience of playing such a role to a wider audience. Each Christmas he dressed as Santa Claus, hired the village hall and entertained his growing work force and their families. In summer – rather like W.S. Gilbert and Arthur Sullivan before him – he would hire a Mears steamer for a day on the Thames. Coaches would take the workers, their wives and children to Hampton Court pier in mid-morning and meet them again in the evening at Windsor.

That was the genial smile of the paterfamilias. Even as visitors we'd glimpse, from time to time, the thunderous tyranny of Mr Barrett of Wimpole Street. I soon recognised that, having seen – in common with most of the family – Charles Laughton with Norma Shearer in action at one of our local cinemas.

To his four growing children Uncle William must have seemed, very often, an ogre who embodied retribution and evinced terror. They were not studious youngsters. Whenever one of them attempted anything that was humorous in a childish way, the beetle brows would tower over him, the fleshy jowls turn puce and the culprit would be enjoined to find a book and educate himself. There was no space for laughter in that house. Unfavourable comparisons were made with me, since I was doing well at school. My parents would say nothing but I'd wink covertly at my cousins and we'd remain friends despite the storms.

To my cousin Audrey, her father showed a wary indulgence. Maybe this was because there'd been a second daughter who'd died in infancy: the survivor was cosseted a little. To John and Michael and Graham their father was, too often, a tyrant no matter how frequent or large the cheques paid out to private schools and tutors who'd attempt to instil a scholarship for which they'd neither enthusiasm nor aptitude.

24

The latest expensive toys and gadgets from Hamleys may have impressed them for an hour. It did not buy their affection. It was not for me to persuade them to do as I imagined I would have done. Young heroes in my Robert Louis Stevenson novels would have been my guide in like circumstances. I would have upped and off. My cousins did not escape until later and then in very different ways.

John, my favourite, was eight years older than myself. Gentle, blue-eyed like his mother, soft-spoken and with an uncomplicated affection for me, he stayed at home as his father's chauffeur until he was called up in September 1939. Within a year he was killed instantly at Dunkirk when the truck he was driving was shelled.

For months after, his father would haunt the arrival platforms at Charing Cross and London Bridge, handing cigarettes and bars of chocolate to returning soldiers, questioning them in hope of information about the death of his eldest son. William's grief was sincere. It seemed quite untainted by the late Victorians' gift for play-acting: bereaved parent, good-hearted tears at family reunions after a row, and all the rest of their self-deluding garbage.

Later in the war, Audrey eloped from her father's more modest house near Epsom Station with a Canadian soldier billeted nearby. She really did elope. Bright girl, she understood Mr Barrett's language and answered him in it. Michael, too, disappeared one evening, joined the Merchant Navy and wrote only when he'd reached the sanctuary of an Australian port.

Nervous and hysterical Graham, the runt of the litter, was never able to summon enough confidence during adolescence to assert himself and make a break for it. The option of coming to terms with his father just withered. Poor Graham became mildly schizoid. At first he was a voluntary patient in one of the many hospitals set among the North Downs. Later he became a long-stayer in a home for nervous diseases.

Divorced from Aunt Renée on grounds of incompatibility, and with his four children gone, William Robinson moved restlessly around the south of England. He changed houses as frequently as he changed his housekeeper-companions. That was my mother's evasive way of referring to the succession of ex-waitresses, former secretaries and one-time senior shop assistants who waited to welcome us on later visits. William's charm did not diminish in old age. When he was seventy-two his current housekeeper had to make a brief but rapid trip to a discreet nursing home. My mother was dismissive but my persistent questions pushed her to tight-lipped embarrassment.

William himself moved on and on in an endless quest for contentment that his dwindling bank balance could not buy. There was Raynes Park, then Bournemouth, Richmond, Effingham and Stoneleigh. When his money ran out, so did the last of the seventeen housekeepers. He spent his final Christmas in a bedsitter in Eastbourne. Having cooked his own lunch, he ate it, pulled two crackers and placed the paper hats on his own head and his cat's. Within months he died leaving ten pounds in a Post Office Savings Book.

Aunt Renée was among his few mourners. I was not. On the day of his funeral I thought of Chaffer's Mead: its spaciousness, its affluence and its chilly Gothic overtones.

TO AUNT MARGE

–Theatrical? No, I wouldn't describe her playing as that. . .
My mother paused and I knew she was thinking over my
question. I was using a newly-acquired adjective for the first
time and she was considering its suitability. She glanced first
at my father and my brother. Then she looked well beyond
them, appearing to study the cruiser-grey waves of the Solent
as they lapped closer to us over the oily pebbles.
We were finishing a couple of plates of cockles at the time,
sheltered from a westerly breeze by the weathered superstruc-
ture of the Clarence Pier. Having wiped each of her fingers in
turn on a linen handkerchief, my mother looked at me again
and delivered her assessment of Margery's performance at the
piano the previous evening:
–No, it wasn't theatrical. She plays with the flashiness one
would expect in a four-ale bar. Not that I have ever been in
a four-ale bar.
This was her judgement on a friend she'd known for fifteen
years, someone in whose home we were staying and the
woman who had become godmother to her younger son.
My mother ante-dated Edith Evans's performance as Lady
Bracknell by more than a decade. With the film and stage
productions of *The Importance Of Being Earnest* over, Dame
Edith redirected her talents and played other roles. Not so my
mother. She lived the part of Lady Bracknell, though she'd not
read a word of Wilde. No actress, however great, could hope
to have been more than my mother's understudy.
It's possible that my mother's cultivated poise, coupled with
her Highland ancestors' directness and her evident knowledge
of nineteenth-century fiction might have presented to Aunt
Marge a persona that she found irresistible. This lonely

27

romantic who, for many years, I supposed to be a blood relative, was no such thing. It was some time, too, before I realised that the name Margery appeared neither on her birth certificate nor her passport.

Rosetta Marjoram was one of three children born to a cockney couple who had, for most of their working lives, kept a boarding-house in Brighton. They'd retired to Portsmouth where they rented a terraced house in Princes Street, just off the Commercial Road and a little to the north of the house where Charles Dickens had been born.

Sometime in 1919, before sailing with my father to India, my mother had spent a few days in Queen Charlotte's Hospital, Portsmouth. We were never told why but there was, presumably, some mild uterine problem to be solved.

In the next bed was Rosetta, then working in the accounts office of a bookseller to whom she often referred subsequently: it sounded like Roberts & Rates. Since her diction underwent more and more gentrification as the years passed, that may not have been the spelling.

The two young women found a common interest in books. It's a fair guess that it would have been Aunt Marge who pursued the acquaintanceship beyond the hospital gates. More than a guess if her later, relentless quests for friendship are acceptable evidence. Throughout her life she was over-eager to establish mutual interests with strangers: with those in neighbouring seats at a concert, with the staff at her local cinemas, or with those who happened to be sheltering near her during an air-raid or at a bus stop. On any long journey she travelled invariably by coach for it ensured an intimacy from which at least one fellow passenger couldn't escape. This couldn't be guaranteed in a train.

These numerous overtures were prompted by a blend of loneliness and good intentions. Occasionally they were successful but, far more often, they foundered on acrimonious charges of busybodying before sinking into unhappy silences. That her friendship with my mother lasted until Aunt Marge's death can be attributed only to the geographical distance that separated the two women for most of the year.

In 1919, Rosetta Marjoram was also about to sail away and, for the following seven years, she and my mother corresponded. Letters were exchanged on a monthly basis between Calcutta and Peru. Rosetta had just married a young coffee-planter who'd been back in Portsmouth on home leave. Miss Marjoram – she insisted it be pronounced Marjawrum with the second syllable accented – had become Mrs Norris.

To me, as a child of seven, it was bewildering to have to address her birthday and Christmas cards. How could I write Mrs Norris when I could hear that over-modulated voice referring to Mrs Norrie, little Mrs Shortie and Miss Zeet? She was, by then, in her mid-thirties and her fondness for romanticising herself and others had become a characteristic.

My mother's letters, during the very early years of their friendship, were posted from Howrah just across the Ganges from Calcutta. The replies came from somewhere that Aunt Marge referred to always as Camp. Listening restlessly to her nostalgic anecdotes after breakfast in Princes Street and wondering if we would ever get away to tour Nelson's *Victory* or make for Hayling Island to build sandcastles, I could never quite visualise her in South America.

Images of my parents in India were much clearer, helped by photographs still pinned inside the lids of their sea-chests. These supplemented tales of a world in which they were surrounded by bullock carts, tennis courts, servants who didn't always wash their hands after going to the lavatory, and dinner parties that ended with coffee and mango ices being served on a verandah.

But what could Camp be? At most, it evoked for me the label on bottles of coffee extract that the English, until recently, used as the basis for a hot milky drink. I could only suppose that Aunt Marge and her husband Norrie sat outside a tent, resting from their labours in some steamy jungle, while a turbanned gentleman served them hot drinks at sundown.

I gathered, after the gory details had been relived for us five or six times during as many visits, that Norrie or Shortie or whatever his name was, had developed mastoiditis in Camp and had died in some agony before he could be hospitalised. The most exciting bit, for me, was the tragic journey downriver by raft for the dying man and his wife.

Within days, widowed Aunt Marge sailed for England where she received a pay-out from her husband's employers. By the time she figured in my consciousness, she'd invested this lump sum. She then owned half a dozen terraced cottages

29

in one of Portsmouth's tattier side-streets. This done, she resettled herself in her parents' gaslit and lace-curtained home. With the income derived from her tenants she was able to indulge her romantic interests in films, musicals and Boots' library books.

To these diversions she was able to add the role of comfortably-off aunt. It was one she played to her own nephews and nieces, to my brother and me and – later on – to our cousins and their cousins, too. As she quarrelled with her own kin, she tried her luck – with not much more success – among our own extended family.

It seemed curious to me, as a child, that this woman who had no blood connection with us should be on much closer terms with my Hampshire relatives than I was.

Her financial independence allowed her to descend on us in Twickenham more often than we could visit her in her home setting. My parents, having returned from India, were tied with a young family. My father, whose brilliance as a mechanical engineer was matched only by an unworldliness that would astonish an eight-year-old today, had sailed home in the great slump and was working as a daily-paid hand at a firm in Isleworth. He made liquid batteries for the radio sets that were being produced for an increasingly enthusiastic market. His pay was meagre and he worked overtime whenever he could. We were never hungry but we were poor.

So it was not possible, in those years immediately preceding World War II, for us to go on holiday as a family. My father, rather like freelance workers today, was paid only for the hours he put in. My first trips to Princes Street were with my mother and my brother. My father would appear only at the end of the week, having travelled straight from the factory in his working clothes on Saturday afternoon.

He would have seen us off, of course, the previous weekend at Waterloo, waving goodbye until the steam train had curved out of sight to begin its three-hour journey. I was never bored. I'd a book and, if I tired of it, there was the mosque to look out for at Woking, the long tunnel south of Guildford in which coal-smuts from the engine would blacken our faces unless we closed the window, and at last the strangely clean white walls of small houses in Portsmouth's northern suburbs.

At the Town Station Aunt Marge would be waiting to meet us. She was easily identified among the crowd by a dash of heliotrope, lilac or mauve that was an integral part of any of her countless outfits. Fresh violets might be pinned to her coat or velvet ones stitched under the brim of her hat. We'd spot her soon enough. There would be the luxury of a taxi that was, to my eyes, the best the provinces could manage. However spacious the limousine, it could hardly emulate the snug privacy of one of London's black cabs.

As we were driven north from the Guildhall Square, I'd have my first glimpse of those open-topped buses on which I'd be able to travel to the beach for a ha'penny. And there'd just be time before our car swung under the railway bridge to check that my favourite ice-cream parlour was still in business. This was very important: was there still the chance of enjoying a knickerbocker glory topped with pineapple chunks and a glacé cherry, price sixpence?

Our route took us between the new chain stores that were opening along the Commercial Road. Aunt Marge's prattle, begun on the station platform, continued:

–We've got our own Timothy White's now, you see . . . and you see that new Burton's? Remember when that was a whole row of what I always called sailors' bars? . . . They're planning an extension of our Portsea Island Co-op there. . .

The commentary was addressed to my mother. I did remember a series of bars with open doors but it was many years before I cracked the euphemism. I was not too young, however, to have become aware of Aunt Marge's civic pride in the city she referred to as Pompey. Her interest in housing, drains, transport and parks would have fitted her to be an editorial adviser to the local evening paper.

It was not merely the door of 6, Princes Street that was familiar to me. There was a distinctive smell, once that door was opened. Whatever the day, there was the thick and cloying odour of washing being boiled in the kitchen copper and a slightly sweet overtone from huge suet puddings simmering on a wood stove.

Not until we'd unpacked and were drinking tea in her mother's overheated kitchen would Aunt Marge home in on her emotional interests: our relatives, neighbours and even the shop-keepers in our local parade at home. They peopled the script of her imaginative existence like walk-ons, yet each had the potential for a larger or star role. Their misfortunes, their errant children, their ailments and their romances: Aunt Marge hungered for details, pouncing on trivial developments as the script-writers of soap operas must do today.

On the pretext of sending a Christmas or Get Well card, she'd elicit an address from my mother. Overnight some reason for making instant contact would be fabricated: a card would be sent next day. A mere signature below some banal verses never sufficed. The whole card would be covered, back, sides and margins with an effusive letter. Jokey cuttings from newspapers and magazines would be enclosed. These were her stepping-stones. Should there be anything more than the barest acknowledgement, then another regular correspondence leading on to a new port of call in Twickenham would have been established. To Aunt Marge, letter writing was a growth industry. It enabled her to play agony aunt whether her counsel was needed or not. In her mother's eyes, it at least kept her daughter out of the way for the major part of the morning.

Grandma Marjoram was a kind-hearted, unaffected Victorian housewife and landlady. Even before she was widowed, I can never recall her being dressed in anything other than unpatterned black, navy blue or plain chocolate brown. On those summer mornings when I went shopping with her to Charlotte Street Market, she'd wear a coal-scuttle hat that she'd bought at the end of the First World War and, over her plain frock, a flowered wrap-around apron. She continued to wear this despite daily protests from Aunt Marge. The real objection was never voiced though easily guessed. Grandma Marjoram had no interest in upward mobility. The apron was never removed other than on Sunday evenings. Aunt Marge pleaded to no avail. She tried addressing her mother as Momma but the only response was a glassy stare. When Aunt Marge began to gentrify Princes Street to Princes Terrace, the old lady would raise her grizzled eyebrows, pocket a Woolworth's dictionary in her apron and waddle away to the kitchen to work on one of her *News Of The World* prize crossword puzzles.

As a child, I rather loathed having my hair washed. When I discovered that Grandma Marjoram had never washed her hair in her life but, instead, rubbed coconut oil vigorously into her scalp each Friday evening, I argued passionately for similar treatment. In vain. What doctors recommended for one person, I was told, would not suit another. Force majeure prevailed but I wasn't convinced. At seventy-three the old lady hadn't one grey hair and, remarkably, she exuded no offensive smell.

Plump, and moving with a memorable stateliness, Grandma Marjoram would serve us breakfast in the back parlour. She knew her younger daughter well enough and could be sure Aunt Marge would linger over a third pot of tea, chattering on and on until my own impatience became too evident. Grandma Marjoram left me to win that battle in the back parlour. No way was she going to have her kitchen table occupied by us until eleven o'clock or even noon.

Long after the Kellogg's Cornflakes, the plates of fried eggs, mushrooms, bacon, sausages, tomatoes, bread and sauté potatoes had been eaten, removed and washed, Aunt Marge would continue her discourse on the relatives of her relatives we'd never met. Or, just as often, she'd expand on the cruel cost of maintaining her terraced properties. Cruel was a favourite adjective. As though fearing that we'd remain unimpressed, she'd reinforce its impact by contracting her eyebrows and giving an extra protrusion to her bulbous violet eyes.

She'd a sister and a brother, both married. With both, or with their spouses she'd had, early in my childhood, the most tremendous rows. One rift – with her brother and his Canadian wife – lasted only a few years. That with her sister and brother-in-law was never really patched up. The details of its beginnings were embroidered in the retelling and it was only Aunt Marge's version to which we had access. Nevertheless, her version of the rupture with Sis Ivy and brother-in-law Ralph was sufficiently unedited for us to glean that well-meaning Margie – another variant on her name – had only herself to blame. Again.

Lacking interest in such wrangles, impatient to make for the beach with my shrimping-net and rubber swimming-tyre, I remember mainly the vehemence with which Aunt Marge outlined her case. There was the sweeping contralto, coupled with operatic gestures, that seemed essential to any of her anecdotes. Her fascination with the cinema dated from the era of silent films and the influence of larger-than-life acting was evident.

On a narrow strip of sand by the hot walls of Sally Port or on the shingle by the South Parade Pier, I'd reproduce these bravura performances later in the day with my mother as audience. She'd try to restrain me but only half-heartedly.

–I hinted to Ralphie that he should consider. . .

That is how the row had begun. Ralphie, it seemed, had not listened to his sister-in-law and had thoughtlessly ignored her wagging finger. Within weeks, the suggestion had strengthened:

–I told Ralphie with all the force at my command. . .

Still he was not daunted.

So, during what was to be Aunt Marge's last visit to his house, she'd shouted:

–I order you to. . .

That had been more than enough for the leathery-complexioned man who'd travelled south from Newcastle in search of work, found it at Portsmouth Dockyard and then married his landlady's daughter, Sis Ivy. Poor Margie Rosetta Zeet Shortie Norris Marjoram was ordered out of that cottage in the shadow of Wharf Lane's gasworks and told to stay out.

The following Christmas approached. In the city of Charles Dickens's birth and at a time when the more insidious tentacles of the family could be most effectively used by emotional blackmailers, Aunt Marge embarked on a rapprochement. Cards were sent. Silence was the reply.

In each of the ensuing years she sent birthday gifts to her growing nephews and nieces. She idled at their school gates in snow or shine. After the briefest of hellos they'd scamper away. She cultivated one of their neighbours in Wharf Lane but it was no go the Swiss Ambassador ploy.

A decade passed. Maybe through that same neighbour, maybe through her regular scrutiny of the *Portsmouth Evening News*, Aunt Marge learned of the forthcoming marriage of her eldest niece. A wedding gift was sent. There was no acknowledgement and no invitation. Unrebuffed, Aunt Marge dredged every clothes cupboard and set off to the distant church where she stood at the back like a lilac overburdened with blossom. In a moment worthy of Hollywood at its most tacky, she stepped tearfully into the aisle to confront bride and groom

34

as they returned from signing the register. She touched her niece's forearm. The girl recoiled in a way that she'd certainly not done when, as six-year-olds, she and I had explored each other's bodies in the protective shadow of the gasholders.

Aunt Marge called a cab and, having wept all the three miles back to Princes Street, took to her bed for the remainder of the weekend. Grandma Marjoram, who *had* been invited to the wedding, carried trays of food and Sunday papers up to her daughter.

Glad of some respite from that voice, she worked in the kitchen on her Fashion Competitions and her prize cross-words.

This particular feud was pre-eminent among those that were rehearsed for us after breakfast on every visit we made. We could have prompted the next lines, even mouthed them with Aunt Marge in much the same way that she, some years on, sat watching *The Sound of Music* for the seventeenth time while conducting a singalong with dear Christopher and dear Julie from the stalls.

There was some comfort for me, however, as I listened impatiently at the breakfast table. Her repertoire had a certain predictability. I could sit ticking off the episodes of the major sagas as they were concluded. Having exhausted those tales in which there'd been some fresh developments, Aunt Marge would be forced back on mere repetition. I'd a fair memory and could sense the moment to make my bid for freedom.

As the word-for-word reiteration of some old injustice ended, I'd tap my sandals against my bucket and spade. My mother got the message. It was now or almost never since Aunt Marge, after a minimal pause to fortify herself with the dregs in the teapot, was ready to begin anew.

My mother too, by eleven thirty, felt that we had paid our dues. To have been a captive audience for three hours seemed a reasonable settlement for free board and lodgings.

The Clarence Pier was on a direct tram or trolleybus route from Princes Street. When very small, I much preferred this part of the beach to the South Parade Pier. There was a funfair with miniature clay footballers on sticks ready to kick for goal. There was a ghost train too, and candyfloss stalls and a helter-skelter. From the base of the pier itself, small wherries could be hired and one could bob around in the shallows.

The South Parade Pier, by contrast, entailed a lengthy trudge past the castle or through Southsea Common. In a rare admission of humanity, my mother told me that she'd once walked out on this open parkland with young naval officers. She added – mysteriously at the time – that she'd heard one young sprig warning another he'd best not try his luck with her for Miss Elizabeth Robinson was no flighty bit of stuff.

It was very close to the South Parade Pier that I first became aware of venereal disease. I was seven at the time. I had been dared by my father to piss in the sea while swimming. Though I protested that everyone could see other kids doing just that without bothering to wade in to stomach level, I was defeated. What seemed natural enough to me was, it seemed, a vulgar back-street habit not to be encouraged.

So I made for the gentlemen's toilet to the left of the Pier. Having entered, I had to observe my father's second injunction:

–Never, ever hang around in a public urinal. Do your business; wash your hands and leave.

Supposing this to be yet some other habit that needed to be curbed in respectable suburbia, I normally complied. It was a notice on the wall – scarlet capitals on a white ground – that fascinated and delayed me on that occasion. There was a new word on offer and some perplexing instructions.

The advice must have been aimed at ratings on leave for Portsmouth was then Britain's second largest naval station. Should anyone, I read, have reason to think he might have been infected with a venereal disease, he should immediately immerse his member in a solution of permanganate of potash. Very odd indeed. Why such instructions in a gentlemen's toilet?

Potassium permanganate was familiar enough. It was the base of that purple solution my grandmother kept hidden in a cupboard so that she could mask her greying hair with a nut-brown tint. The only member of which I was then aware was the Member of Parliament for Twickenham, my grandmother's acquaintance, Mr Edward Keeling.

I left the loo imagining that rather prim and worthy Conservative steeped in purple water and beginning to resemble a ripe chestnut. Would he have remembered to remove his horn-rimmed glasses? Had he done so, how could a cold bath cure what I pronounced to myself as vernal disease? It was not a problem about which I could consult my parents. Anything concerning that part of our bodies between the neck and the knees was never a conversational topic in our family.

Throughout my childhood it was impossible for me to bridge the chasm between what I learned of physiology in the corners of the school playground and the silences and evasions with which birth and sex were treated at home. Consequently, a song Aunt Marge included in her repertoire during musical evenings embarrassed me acutely. Musical evenings were an inescapable part of our visits.

It was on Saturday night usually, when my father had arrived to take us home the following day, that Aunt Marge's ringed fingers would twinkle a glissando along the piano keys. She was warming up. A selection of ballads, numbers from current musicals and arias from the more popular operas would follow. From the very first arpeggio I waited in dread for *Trees*. I could spot that dog-eared sheet of music long before she tweaked it from between *I dreamt that I Dwelled In Marble Halls* and *Vilia*. As her thumb and forefinger closed on it I would get up and creep swiftly from the front parlour. I'd whisper to my mother that I needed to go to the lavatory in the back yard. As proof I'd take with me a torch from a corner table. This would dispel the shadows that lurked between the coal-shed and the hen-house. It cannot have been many months before my mother made the connection between my exit and the ballad but it wouldn't have been in her nature to comment. The impossible line:

. . . the earth's sweet flowing breast. . .

occurred half-way through.

Breast, like b-t-m, belly-button and fart were never mentioned though I knew them all, and more. Even at Christmas, if an uncle – jolly with light ale as he carved the turkey –thoughtlessly asked my mother if she'd care for a bit off the breast, he'd be given an Arctic smile such as Lady Bracknell might have bestowed on an over-familiar porter. There'd be a pause no longer than a heart-beat and then my mother would reply:

–A little of the white meat will do well enough, thank you.

Of course, I went nowhere near the lavatory in Princes Street. I stood in the cluttered passage that led to the street door waiting for the song to end. When it had done I'd return to the parlour. It was a hazardous business, making my way back to my fireside stool. I had to negotiate a path between immense and sombre ornamental jars that stood at vantage points around the room. Each one of them was large enough to conceal Ali Baba or any of his forty thieves. Then came the final terror: a puma skin that served as a mat. Long dead the beast may have been before Aunt Marge brought it back as a trophy from Peru. True, I could see well enough that the eyes were no more than painted glass marbles but, to a seven-year-old, those open fangs were terrifying.

My ordeal over for another visit, I'd relax as the amateur recital continued. Aunt Marge would accompany Sis Ivy – or she did until they were no longer on speaking terms. Sis Ivy whistled as well as sang. She'd perform *Sally* using a mixture of both quite as nimbly as Gracie Fields could ever have done.

Though Grandma Marjoram was slightly deaf – an impediment she used to advantage when subjected for too long to Aunt Marge's barrages of advice – she appeared interested in the entertainment her daughters provided. Well, she'd at least look on until, either soothed by the music or exhausted by a long day in the kitchen, she'd nod off in her armchair and snore. Her husband preferred other entertainment. After supper and well before the piano-lid had been lifted, he made for a local bar to see what was on offer; the four-ale bar, maybe.

This fierce old man who slurped his breakfast tea through a moustache cup had, I felt, a dubious sense of humour. I probably deserved to be the target of his jokes for I'm certain I stared rudely and incredulously at him as he drank. He'd look up at me when I least expected it:

–As for you, young shaver, I'll chop off yer head and screw on a cauliflower instead.

I was very wary of Grandpa Marjoram.

He offered repeatedly to take me on a secret expedition. It was one that would have made blackberrying on Hayling Island or canoeing at Hillsea tame by comparison. I was – just as secretly – grateful that the opportunity never seemed to occur. Maybe it was no longer available: perhaps no more than a memory the old man had stored after a visit to some

travelling fair decades before. Yet he still urged me, on every visit, to set aside a few coppers from my holiday money:
–You'll need tuppence, young shaver. I'll show you a woman who'll bite off a live rat's head for tuppence.

My mother, while deploring what she termed Mr Marjoram's coarseness, privately admired his plainspokenness. She found it preferable to the ever-more-mannered speech and gestures of his daughter.

It was from my mother that I learned of the old man's favourite relaxation in the local bars. She could hardly have learned it from Aunt Marge who would have been horrified. It's possible my father may have accompanied him now and again. Until well into his sixties, it seems, old George Marjoram would down as many pints as he could pay for. Well tanked up but still thirsty, he'd throw his cap into the air and offer to fight any man in the bar for a drink.

Sometime late in the decade the old man died. Grandma Marjoram took a regular lodger again not only for company's sake. The household had become less prosperous because Aunt Marge was beginning to feel the pinch. Her terraced cottages were becoming less of a source of income; more a liability. The tenants' demands for repairs became noisy and frequent. For the first time she had to draw on her invested capital and her round of visits to friends and contacts became noticeably more protracted, especially in winter. On one occasion she arrived at our house with a woman friend, bringing a bunch of flowers for my mother, fifty cigarettes for my father and a wooden toy grenadier for me. The visitors stayed six weeks and my mother's friendship with Aunt Marge underwent some strain.

Comparatively straitened circumstances impelled her to dig herself in more resolutely with my father's relatives who still lived in and around Portsmouth.

She set about cultivating their relatives, too. With this in mind, she campaigned for a distant uncle – a man I scarcely knew – when he first contested a seat on the City Council. Years later she was outside Buckingham Palace when, having made it to Lord Mayor, the said uncle was decorated with a C.B.E. Though we knew nothing of the subsequent celebration, Aunt Marge was in on the champers.

And then old Grandma Marjoram died. It was wartime.

Portsmouth had been blitzed and Princes Street irreparably damaged. Aunt Marge had prudently sold her cottages just after Munich and both mother and daughter lived in furnished accommodation on the northern edge of the city.

Having for the first months of the war reviled both the government and the country that had forced her to capitalise her investment in property:

–England? She needn't count on me in her need. What has this land ever done for me? I'm a widow reduced to penury. . .

she changed overnight after the Luftwaffe's first heavy raids on the Dockyard. She got patriotism like a bug.

Through some string-pulling at the Guildhall – thanks to the Lord Mayor – she was given war work as counsellor to Portsmouth's unmarried mums. All was well for a couple of years but then her over-identification syndrome took charge again. She was first at the office in the morning, treading daintily through broken glass and shrapnel, and she was last to leave. She became increasingly critical of the whole system and was certain she could overhaul it. Her tide of letters to superiors went unanswered. Finally, at a Guildhall reception, she told the Medical Officer of Health that his policies were both cruel and inhuman. Like her brother-in-law years earlier he showed her to the steps.

Undeterred she made her way back to the Lord Mayor's Parlour within a couple of months. This time my distant uncle found her another, less public, niche. She became housekeeper to the chairman of a parish council just outside Portsmouth. The sprightly widower didn't expect much of Aunt Marge's cooking – which was just as well – but he did have expectations in the bedroom. When he left a packet of condoms lying on the bedside table she became agitated but continued dusting and said nothing. On her sixtieth birthday, her employer's kiss was more than friendly. She locked herself in the lounge, howled for an hour and then rang the long-suffering Lord Mayor.

Back on the cocktail party circuit once more, she met an eighty-year-old county alderman: another widower and a prominent freemason. To the irritation of his children and grandchildren, she married him. This late autumn romance lasted exactly six months. To the alderman's bewilderment it was never consummated. A goodnight cuddle at the top of the stairs was all that Aunt Marge was prepared to offer. Whether this was too little or too much for the alderman we never discovered. She found him dead on the doormat one April morning and inherited his very comfortable home near Copnor Bridge.

Her mourning was brief. Soon she began to concentrate her emotional interests on a series of younger women. In adolescence I began to wonder whether there might have been an unrealised lesbianism in Aunt Marge. Her friendships were passionate and possessive. They must often have been bewildering to those young shop assistants and secretaries who were rushed off to concerts at the Guildhall or to the nicer type of tea-shop out Southsea way.

An appalling cook herself, she enjoyed good restaurant food. She'd a fair palate for a fine sherry, too, and knew where one could be found. Her knowledge of the Portsmouth pubs was not confined to four-ale bars, whatever my mother thought. Aunt Marge would indicate tactfully to me, when I visited her as a young adult, those that were for gentlemen only and the one or two that were frequented by lonely young naval officers on leave.

Concerts and restaurants provided her with enjoyable outings but it was the cinema that nourished her romanticism. Just how early in life she began to identify with Bette Davis it's impossible to say. O yes, she bought and sang those songs that had been popularised on the screen by Grace Moore. Certainly she wept with Scarlett O'Hara and reread *Gone With The Wind* until she had the script by heart. But it was Bette Davis who, all unawares, coached Aunt Marge in the authoritative glance and that telling flash of the bulbous eyes.

If only Bette Davis had not signed to play Elizabeth the Virgin Queen. Aunt Marge was never quite the same after following the actress's every nuance through at least seven performances. Or maybe she was the same – but more so. True, Miss Davis wore an auburn wig and Aunt Marge still had her own hair but there was decidedly less of it each year. I knew that early on, for I'd peep at her through the open door as she dressed.

The girlish plaits were looped and coiled around her brow each morning in an ever more intricate stratagem. It became progressively more difficult for her to conceal the secret:

41

there was little more than a sparse root or two on top. She adopted a nightcap. No courtiers i.e. neighbours, home help or protégées, were admitted until she'd put on what she termed her Sunday or Monday or Thursday face. Echoes of the film became louder. Then, when she was ready for the day, her manner – post-Bette – grew more grand as she served us cups of weak instant coffee. As for her turn of phrase, my father had it about right:

–She sounds like Shakespeare in a village hall.

There were less formal moments. She was still nimble enough at seventy-two to step it out along the promenade from Southsea to Sally Port for a breath of evening air, pausing only for a reviving schooner of sherry and a round of turkey sandwiches at a half-way stop.

But her contemporaries were beginning to die off. She was most affected by the deaths of three members of my own family in quick succession. We had become her adopted kith and kin. The long romance with us – or the us she'd invented in her imagination – was over.

Hearing that she'd a mild autumn chill we drove to Copnor to see her. My youngest aunt took one look at Marge, tottering in front of us in a quilted dressing-gown, then whispered to me:

–We'll never see her alive again.

She was right. Aunt Marge had decided that the witch doctor's bones were pointing at her. She told her own doctor she'd no wish to recover from what was no more than a mild indisposition.

Instead, having led us to her bedroom that afternoon, she began to enact a grand Act Four. Bette Davis, it's true, kept to historical tradition and played the death of Elizabeth standing up, whereas Aunt Marge took to her bed. Secondary influences must be taken into account: those matinée performances of *Traviata* and *Bohème* at the King's Theatre, Southsea, had left their mark.

She rested on five pillows and the lace window-curtains were drawn. The light from a bedside lamp – softened by a ruched lilac shade – was kinder to her features than the sunshine over Portsmouth that afternoon would have been. The skin that we'd never been permitted to see unlacquered appeared – despite the subdued lighting – a mass of scrunched blotting-paper.

She sipped a glass of sherry. Then with my mother, my aunt, the home help and me as audience, she drew off her rings one by one. She offered a particularly flash dress ring to me. I thought of the original Elizabeth I and of her ring being borne away to Scotland by some young knight who offered it to gay James in Edinburgh. The comparison broke down: I'd no James around me at the time to whom I'd wish to give it, so I refused.

It was redistributed, with the rest, among the onlookers. Our genuine protests that she would be up and about and off to a concert by the weekend were waved aside. She sighed, finished her sherry and shook a few bizarrely pinned curls out of place. The rings and other mementoes distributed, she sent the women to the kitchen to make tea. In a frail and halting voice, she dictated her will.

We told her again, before we all left, that the whole thing was a nonsense. We assured her that one or two of us would be back in a couple of days and stay for the weekend. The following morning the home help phoned me. Aunt Marge, drinking her breakfast tea, had put down her cup, closed her eyes, sighed once more and was gone.

Theatrical? Most certainly. As I said to my mother after the funeral, Marge gave a finer performance than anything you'd see in a four-ale bar.

TO *THE DOLPHIN*

were less frequent than visits to Aunt Marge, though they were not unconnected.

Whenever we stayed at Princes Street we'd make a day trip to *The Dolphin* and vice versa. *The Dolphin* is still in Havant, half an hour by bus from Portsmouth or a couple of stops north of the city on the slow trains bound for London. It's a double-fronted building that stands in East Street, a few steps from the crossroads of the little Hampshire market town.

Between the two World Wars my father's middle brother and his wife managed this early nineteenth-century hotel between them. It was always rather more than a pub and, during summer months, the half dozen bedrooms were let to holidaymakers. We could hardly expect to stay there on the cheap in the high season so our visits to my uncle and aunt – who could not easily leave their work – were day trips only.

There was one recurring problem: Aunt Marge. How to prevent her coming to Portsmouth Town Station on the pretext of seeing us off and then, with a seemingly impromptu gesture, buying a bunch of flowers as a gift and including herself in for the day? It became apparent to my parents after a year or so that Aunt Marge might not be as welcome at *The Dolphin* as she supposed herself to be. I gathered that she had been trying to put lunch or tea at Havant on her roster of weekly visits. My mother attempted a gentle deterrent at breakfast:

–We're only going for a few hours. Shouldn't think we'll stay for more than a cup of tea. After all, what this young man really wants is the sands at Hayling Island. Besides, they'll be busy this time of year. Run off their feet serving lunches. They won't want us hanging around. . .

It worked for a couple of summers and then Aunt Marge replied brightly that she'd come anyway.

The problem was solved when my father was taken on staff at work. No longer having to take unpaid holidays as a daily hired hand, he could join us for a whole week. Provided we varied visits between autumn and April we could stay at Havant.

My father liked the town with its cattle-market, its egg-grading station and the little roads leading from the built-up area to woodlands he'd known since adolescence. Quite often I'd go with him on one of his five-mile walks. In Westbourne Woods he'd tell me the names of trees that did not grow in Twickenham and birds far more colourful and fascinating than the commonplace sparrows, thrushes and starlings that flitted through our apple trees.

I found such outings instructive and interesting. They could never have been as exciting, though, as the expeditions I made with my cousin Norman, seven years my senior. He'd sit me on the crossbar of his cycle and then we'd venture as far as Bosham Harbour with our nets. Once there, we'd gather buckets of cockles for his mother, Aunt Maud, to cook in a great aluminium pan in the kitchen of *The Dolphin*.

Compared with our own hotels along the Thames, *The Dolphin* seemed to me more of a rambling house set in its own estate. True, the Thameside hotels had gardens otherwise I'd never have been taken to them but those behind the hotel in Havant stretched on and on.

From the rear of *The Dolphin* a covered way led to a huge barn roofed with corrugated iron. I'd sit in this, listening to rain pounding down much as it must have done – I then supposed – on the roof of Noah's Ark. But I remember that barn just as vividly on cloudless afternoons. Aunt Maud would be setting out plate after plate of sandwiches and cakes on trestle tables. Soon enough the cricketers would crowd in after a match and then that great space would be filled from rafters to floorboards with endless anecdotes and laughter.

If I crossed a sandy yard to the right, there was the Tap Room. This was opened only in the evenings. Old men, locals, would relax there, sipping one pint of pale ale, making it last till closing time while they played cribbage or pondered a next move with their dominoes. There was never much money taken at that bar. Aunt Maud smiled when I mentioned this:

–That's not the point, my dear. It's a haven for them, you see. They don't need to dress up to come in here. Just so long as they've washed the farm muck from their hands and boots, they're welcome.

Beyond the Tap, set at right angles to it, were stables that dated from the coaching days. My uncle parked his car there as did those few pre-war visitors who arrived by road. Over the stables was a vast hayloft which I could reach by ladder. It was there, among the full potato sacks and watched by an occasional curious mouse, that my cousin Norman taught me to play darts.

On sunny mornings, when he was at school working for something mysterious called Matric., I'd wander further. Beyond the forlorn stables and through a painted wooden gate there was the bowling green and its pavilion. Further still, the tennis courts. Only when I'd passed these and sampled a few unripe blackberries on hedges bounding the kitchen garden, would I come to a high ragstone wall capped with orange tiles. In one corner of it was a locked gate. By the time I'd grown tall enough to stretch up and turn the key, I knew there'd be no magic landscape of undiscovered woods beyond. The gate led to a narrow lane – just a short cut to the station.

Within the hotel itself there were bars to the left and right of a flagged entrance hall. On all but stormy mornings the heavy street-door was propped open so that the fug of tobacco and the flat, sour smell of beer built up overnight could escape.

I'd stand in that hall and watch my Uncle Ted rising from a trap door that led down to the cellars. He'd come into view like a coalman or a miller with a load that weighed him almost double. On each of his seven or eight trips he'd bring up a full barrel of Hampshire ale or cider.

It was in the larger of the two bars that I recall standing one night, dared into silence, after the towels had been hung across the brass pump handles. To the cursory glance of any passer-by, closing time had been observed and the licensing laws respected. That particular night no one was drinking Alton ales and there were no towels over the whisky and gin bottles. Aunt Maud's brother had, that evening, been elected to Portsmouth City Council. Our holiday coincided with the election so we joined in the celebration. Aunt Marge was there, too. She'd been out all week canvassing for the Conservative cause and for a man she had, at that time, hardly met.

I stood with my mother's hand over my mouth. It was easy for me to hold my breath. I'd learned to do that when passing a tramp who coughed and spat his way along the pavement near my school. My class-mates had advised me to hold my breath as a precaution against catching his tuberculosis. A celebration at *The Dolphin* was rather different but I played possum all the same and gripped my lemonade very firmly. I'd no wish to be the cause of my uncle losing his licence.

Presumably some look-out had been posted. Someone must have been by the curtained windows that gave onto East Street, watching for the night-duty policeman. No doubt the constable's patrol on his bicycle was predictably regular. The all-clear was given at last and it was safe for the party to continue. I could risk munching some of the Smith's Crisps with which I'd been bribed – could even dare to unwrap the screw of oiled blue paper in the corner of the bag and salt them.

The hotel kitchen was to the rear of this larger bar. It was there that I wept after I'd wrenched my ankle on a cycling expedition to collect bluebells. I was consoled by relatives, particularly my cousin, who felt responsible. I was eight and he was fifteen. He'd a collection of birds' eggs, World War I medals, girlfriends and adventure books. I adored him. Even the slight body odour from those overworked adolescent glands couldn't make him unattractive: maybe the reverse.

My wrenched ankle was bathed in warm water, painted with witch hazel solution and firmly bound. To cheer me up by appealing to my supposed interest in history (an interest my grandmother and my mother had done much to inflate), I was told a story that's not been confirmed for me from any other source until recently.

The storyteller was Aunt Maud's father who seemed always to be seated by the kitchen fire in a wooden rocking-chair. Old Mr Miles had been a successful farmer in North Hampshire or, as the locals would have put it:
-Over to Alton way, he were.
'll assume the old man must have been born in the mid-nineteenth century. I do remember that he stressed the tale

had been related to him as a boy by his own grandfather. That puts the tradition back at least as far as the eighteenth century.

Like all children then – some now, I suppose – I'd heard anecdotes about Queen Elizabeth I. Most of these were connected with Raleigh, Drake, the Spanish Armada and with Elizabeth's parents: the irrascible Henry VIII and the tragic Anne Boleyn. At Junior School the Virgin Queen became less shadowy for me after the makers of Oxo cubes had sent painting books which we could win as prizes. There, together with George Stephenson and Oliver Cromwell, Elizabeth waited in black and white outline for my orange and scarlet crayons to give substance to her hair.

In a way, old Farmer Miles's tale was relevant to that hair. It also touched on something more private; a matter not referred on in school textbooks – Elizabeth's sexuality.

It's well-documented that London, during the early years of the sixteenth century, was subject to periodic outbreaks of plague. To protect King Henry's three surviving heirs, the children were bundled out of the capital into the sweeter air of the countryside. On one such occasion, the old man claimed, young Princess Elizabeth was whisked away too late. She'd been infected shortly before her fifth birthday and in some country house south of the Thames Valley, she died.

Her hosts and her personal staff were terrified. The King was expected to be hunting in the neighbourhood within weeks. What more natural than that he should wish to see his younger daughter? The countryside was combed discreetly for a child of similar age and appearance. A substitute was found and the King duly deceived. He didn't suspect and was never told that the small child he fondled was a boy.

A bizarre tale but not an impossible one. We know from many sources that Elizabeth shaved. I've some mid-nineteenth century playing cards in which she's shown with a distinctive after-six shadow round the chin and jowls. No other queen in the set has this. It's known that she went bald, swore like a trooper and was held to be, in some ways, mannish. Feminists today might protest justifiably that in a world even more male-dominated than our own, any woman would have needed to be male-identified to retain pre-eminence. The only answer is that Elizabeth's elder sister, Mary Tudor, seems

never to have needed to be so. Finally, there's the well-known quip old Farmer Miles did not mention that afternoon in the hotel kitchen. When Elizabeth died and gay James of Scotland was invited to succeed, the courtiers' cry was:
—The King is dead; long live the Queen.
Whatever the basis for the whole story, it intrigued me. It was my first glimpse of a sexuality very different from the apparently ordered lives of the relatives and neighbours who surrounded me as a child.
Just how orthodox were those lives? I began to listen more intently as I appeared to concentrate on a book or toy.
There was always the odd innuendo and some quiet giggling round the supper table during any family get-together at *The Dolphin*. My Uncle Ted was the custodian of family traditions and gossip. He could be depended on to tell a tale wittily even though it might embarrass his mother, my grandmother. No string of reminiscences over the Stilton cheese and celery was complete without an allusion to Mrs Humby, though it was hardly possible that this Dickensian-sounding walk-on could still have been alive. I knew that and so I wondered why my uncle was always so solicitous about her health.
My grandmother, fortified by a glass or so of light ale, would shake her curls and affect ignorance of any such person. She did know, of course, as did all the other adults. Mrs Humby was my grandmother's own mother. She'd run off, I gathered, leaving a husband and four small children, to live on the other side of Portsmouth with a Mr Humby, whoever he may have been. All I know of the pair is what was murmured always at this point in the story by my youngest aunt:
—Married but never churched, my dear.
Divorce on the grounds of infidelity seems never to have been considered by my Great-grandfather Silversmith. When I as old enough to have asked whether he perhaps preferred to enjoy injured martyrdom, there was no one left who could have answered.
A few more minutes, another sip or so of ale, and my uncle would sigh, shake his head and ask about little Eva.
—Is there anyone tending that poor girl's grave?
I didn't know the word tending when I first heard the question. I suspected that tending a girl's grave might be some cloudy allusion to unmentionable things like *private*

49

parts. Later I wondered whether Charles Dickens, through his early association with Portsmouth, had spent time culling names and tear-jerking situations from the raw life of local families, especially my own.

Not so. Little Eva did exist – or she had done. My own father had been sweet on her when he'd been a first-year grammar school boy. So sweet that she'd stuck a note through his letter-box asking if his intentions were serious.

Eva was one of two illegitimate children my grandmother's elder sister had borne to the owner of an hotel in Streatham. He was a Roman Catholic. Great-aunt Frances, an ancient pensioner existing in a bed-sit when I'd been taken to see her, had lived with her man though he'd been unable to divorce his wife. She'd helped manage the hotel and had reared his two children until both had died of tuberculosis in early adolescence.

My grandmother, thoroughly discomposed by this time, would try to divert the conversation. My uncle was not an unkind man. His mother could at last relax as he turned to recollections of his own great-uncle's later years. Robert Clack, messmate, friend and finally brother-in-law of my Great-grandfather Robins had left Queen Victoria's Marines and set up in business somewhere in the oldest part of Portsmouth: close to the harbour from which Nelson once sailed. It's been gentrified today and is a little too picturesque. In 1870 it was very much the rough end of town.

Bob Clack took the lease on a bar where sailors paid the exorbitant sum of a shilling for a pint of beer. That was downstairs in the bar where they were told:

–Collect yer change upstairs, Jack.

And usually Jack did. Upstairs were the girls. The word brothel was never used. But there was always laughter round the table whenever my uncle alluded to someone having a bob (the slang for a shilling).

As the stories tumbled out, I stored the phrases and pondered the laughter. My mother, I noticed early on, would sip an orange juice and listen in pained silence. She preserved a distaste for the frailties of the family into which she had married. This was odd. Her brother's infidelities must have been known to her. Her own mother had eloped for a second marriage: another four children almost abandoned.

50

Her step-brother went to live in Kenya, having fallen in love with a coffee-planter:

–Dye his hair? A man dye his hair? What nonsense. Yes, of course it became blond and curly. Merely the effect of so much travel through the Red Sea . . . after all, he was the cocktail barman on a P & O liner.

And yet she could not condone the failings of those to whom she was not directly related. Ah well, blood's thicker than water, as I was told so often.

It was not only warm April evenings and ripe autumn days that I associate with *The Dolphin*. We celebrated the Christmas of 1937 there. A vast clan gathering it was, not only of my father's family but of Aunt Maud's, too.

Like others in my childhood, that Christmas was a succession of gift-swopping sessions and gargantuan meals. That's not sentimental hindsight. The preparation of food went on for weeks beforehand: the making of pickles, puddings and cakes. None of us had heard of Freud. Had we done so, any theory that we were over-eating to compensate for lack of affection would have been rejected.

A far more plausible explanation for this orgy of eating is historic. Many of my elderly relatives – and the strays who were rounded up for Christmas Day – had known extreme poverty in youth, if not hunger. Meat was for Sundays and holidays. Poultry was bargained for at Saturday-night auctions under the gas flares when street markets were closing. Festivals apart, fruit was a luxury reserved for the sick and the dying. Beer and country wines were home-made and set aside for visitors, while spirits were bought by weekly payments to a Christmas club. Presents, too, were often selected in July or August and paid for by instalments to some neighbour who acted as agent for a mail-order firm.

I can't pretend to recall the particular bedroom in which I slept restlessly that Christmas Eve at *The Dolphin*. I know I shared a large double bed with my grandmother.

Soon after dawn I dived for a pillow-case I'd hung over a brass knob at the foot of the bed the night before. Presents. There were games, of course, and they all looked interesting in their garishly decorated boxes. Best of all, however, there were books. A packaged set of simplified classics was unwrapped immediately. There were six volumes, each in a distinctive rainbow shade of cloth binding: Kingsley's *The Heroes* (red), *Robinson Crusoe* (orange), *Alice in Wonderland* (yellow), *Gulliver's Travels* (green), *Treasure Island* (blue) and *The Swiss Family Robinson* (purple).

I took for granted the assortment of sweets, tangerines, apples and nuts that had percolated to the corners of the pillow-case. The books were the thing. Even before my grandmother stirred, I'd pulled on my dressing-gown cut out from a disused blanket and was deep into the opening chapter of *Treasure Island*.

In less than an hour it was my turn for a bath under the terrifying geyser. This monster, high in one corner of a vast and chilly bathroom, had been activated with a match. After one initial roar, it spat boiling water into a bath that would have accommodated both Laurel and Hardy without discomfort to either. Much to my mother's impatience, I insisted on sitting with my back to the cold water tap. Only in this position could I, like any other wary young animal, face my unpredictable foe.

Christmas Day at *The Dolphin* was one of comparative liberation for me. Had we remained at home I would have been pushed off to sing in the church choir at least three times. At Havant it was sufficient for me to cross East Street and sit in the congregation for Matins with my father and Aunt Marge. Need it be added that she'd arrived by an early bus with Grandma Marjoram?

Back from church and while a chatter of aunts prepared Brussel sprouts, potatoes and every root vegetable available, we'd make our way past the kitchen and up to a rather colourless sitting room on the first floor. Not only the walls but the furnishings, too, were slate grey and an apologetic pale blue. Yes, there was a log fire but it did little to cheer the place. The only really festive touch was a set of Chinese lanterns that hung from an intricate network of wires around the ceiling. These paper globes, the candles in them not yet lit, gave a hint of magic that would come later in the day.

I suspect that Dorothy, my youngest aunt, had felt the need for these decorations since she'd carried them with her from London in a suitcase. They would have revived childhood for her, as well as younger days for my grandmother. The lanterns had been bought for Christmas 1888 and were stored throughout each year in some cupboard or trunk, ready for the next mid-winter.

The sitting room filled gradually with stray unmarried uncles and courtesy aunts who'd either arrived by public transport or were boarding for the holiday with one or other of Aunt Maud's relatives around South Hampshire.

My brother would have been sleeping in his cot and, insofar as he was aware of anything unusual, would have noticed only an increase in the number of fluffy animals that surrounded him. I, as the only child around, was the recipient of small gifts from a succession of callers and distant cousins whose names I scarcely knew.

One such gift that Christmas morning I do remember very clearly – and its donor. He gave me a small puzzle: a flat metallic rectangle with digits enamelled on smaller squares clipped in the frame. One was missing. The trick was to manoeuvre the rest so that the digits ran in sequence either laterally or vertically. I set to work on this immediately yet, absorbed as I was, I can recall the touch of the donor's hand as he ruffled my hair. I can still hear the pitch of that man's voice and the controlled precision of each word as he spoke. I can sympathise now with his extra wariness in showing public affection for a small boy. That Christmas morning, knowing nothing of his inhibitions, my own reaction was one of equal wariness. I'd no wish to sit next to him at lunch.

As we waited for a summons to the table I worked on my new puzzle. Adults chatted about relatives whose names and affairs didn't interest me. Aunt Marge, with my cousin Norman, worked the pianola in the corner and co-operated in a gruff version of Jerome Kern's *Smoke Gets In Your Eyes*.

Perhaps an hour later the whole family could relax. The turkey – including second helpings – had been consumed. Uncles, merry on a whisky or so, made jokes of which I didn't see the point. *God Save The King*, for instance, seemed a fair comment to make when we were about to listen to the anguished stammerings of George VI on the wireless. Yet what could be so amusing about the sotto voce pay-off:

–I've saved him many times, said the chemist.

That condom joke was really inappropriate to the ruling monarch. It must have been an old quip dating from the early years of the century; one far more aptly applied to the profligate Edward VII.

After the jokes there'd be Christmas pudding and mince pies. These were served with brandy butter made by my mother. A Scottish speciality, she'd remind us. Since she was the family's acknowledged authority on anything north of the border, we believed her.

Only then, as extra mince pies were waved aside by those who were diet-conscious, did we pull the Christmas crackers and swop the nonsensical mottoes inside. Apart from miniature musical instruments that seldom worked, the crackers also contained hats. I insisted that these be worn by everybody for the rest of the day. Being the only child among so many adults, I was a little tyrant. Wasn't Christmas Day a festival mainly for children? Well, then. . .

Our dirty crockery removed, the room would grow quiet. My grandmother and those of her generation who'd been excused kitchen duties would begin to snooze noisily. My uncles might attempt a few hands of whist until they, too, settled back to doze. I returned to Jim Hawkins and *Treasure Island* while my cousin was busy flicking through his new encyclopaedia of birds' eggs, comparing the illustrations with his already extensive collection.

I knew what was about to happen: who was expected. As the light became frailer I found it more difficult to read. Relatives dozing nearest me warned that the lamps should not be switched on for fear of waking the sleepers. It was always the same when Father Christmas was expected. Not Santa Claus: he was the one who slipped down the chimney each Christmas Eve. I realised early in life that he was most adept at this for he always avoided getting soot and brick dust on his clothes.

I'm talking about Father Christmas: visible to all and a tangible refutation of all the derisory remarks I heard in my Junior School playground:

–Garn, 'e doesn't exist. It's yer Dad dressed up.

Nonsense. I had seen him; ergo he existed.

Yet that year at *The Dolphin* I was beginning to have private doubts. Every few minutes I double-checked the males in the room. I kept tabs on my father, all my uncles, and the rounded-up strays. But how could I deter my father's youngest brother from going to post letters that he assured me were vital to his job?

–We'll be up late tonight, so I'll get them in the box now and they'll be collected first thing tomorrow morning while we're all still asleep.

–You'll risk missing Father Christmas. . .

–Nonsense. Don't you worry about that. I'll be back in a brace of shakes.

He wasn't of course. Within minutes of the distant street-door slamming – apparently behind him – we could all hear a handbell ringing out in the dusk from somewhere in the direction of the stables. Naturally I was first at the window to catch a glimpse of those scarlet robes edged with cotton wool. Indeed, I was so intent on rushing downstairs and across the gravel to welcome Father Christmas that I must have missed Aunt Maud's quick movement as she disconnected the standard lamps in the sitting room.

Soon he was with us, grunting and puffing his way up the stairs. It was very tiring for him because – I was assured – he was older than any other living being. He certainly uttered a succession of archaic oaths from behind the battered mask that had been bought in 1890 when my father was a toddler.

This annual visit evoked in me as a child a blend of delight and terror. Of course, there was delight that we'd not been forgotten by him on his rounds: far from it, for he always carried half a dozen bulging pillow-cases. But there was terror, too. Though the mask itself was benign enough, Father Christmas was sure to lapse into unearthly cackles as he pranced around the room with saturnalian gusto. There was something supernatural about him. I was apt to confuse him with God the Father and with the Holy Ghost. At church, during the Eucharist, I'd peep between my fingers eager to spot any manifestation of either when the consubstantiation moment was reached. Nothing ever happened above the altar: not a puff of smoke; not a kitten's tongue of fire.

Christmas afternoon was very different – the supernatural was made manifest for me in a sitting room. It was only with tremulous reluctance that I allowed myself to be pushed forward to kiss this apparition. I did accept that it was the least I could offer in return for the mound of gifts he'd brought me. But it was still the uneasiest kiss I ever gave.

When he'd disappeared after refreshing himself with a final guzzle of whisky, the lights were miraculously restored, the Chinese lanterns lit and I could scatter the carpet with torn wrapping paper as I examined my presents. They ranged from the amusing or frivolous, from my grandmother, to the boring but undoubtedly useful from Aunt Gladys. I was so absorbed in checking the gifts and the name tags to discover who might have forgotten me that I was scarcely aware of the return of my missing uncle. I nodded to a small pile of parcels by the fire:

–You've missed him, Uncle. You've only yourself to blame, of course.

During the evening there were guessing games and team games like charades. Everyone on my father's side of the family adored acting. My mother took part reluctantly. After all, she'd said of the Robins family:

–They've amateur theatricals in their blood like a virus.

There were even half-remembered country dances: *Strip the Willow* and *Sir Roger de Coverley*. Refreshment was to hand with all the extravagances associated with Christmas. Our family's traditions were always so well observed that I can state with confidence that there would have been, that year, at *The Dolphin*, bowls of Muscadel grapes mixed with peeled almonds, heaps of pastel-shaded sugared almonds, Turkish Delight, Chinese fig, dates from North Africa and a mound of chestnuts, Brazil nuts, hazels and walnuts.

At nine o'clock we'd a toast to absent friends. I became aware, when very young, that these must include the dead from the expressions of those who towered over me. My father's features assumed their solemn look. There were tears in my grandmother's eyes as she, together with the other adults, recalled previous Christmases dating back decades. For many years I supposed this nine o'clock rite to be something else peculiar to our family and that my uncle Ted had been nominated to propose it. He was always on his feet at the precise moment, whether in his own home or in London. I knew nothing of his connection with freemasonry at the time.

Games and some music continued while supper was being prepared. I recall my grandmother and old Mrs Marjoram, Victorians both, raising their skirts to knee-level in mock musical comedy fashion as they sang *Ten a Penny Walnuts – Taste Before You Buy*.

Cousin Norman ground his way through the almost forgotten ballad *My Old Shako*. And I waited. I knew that I, the family's boy treble, would be cajoled and bribed into singing Mendelssohn's *O For The Wings of a Dove*. Even as a small child I had taken against its rather obvious scoops and swoops. By the time I was fifteen I loathed it. Like so many of the English, my family was adamantly sentimental about pre-pubescent choirboys. They wheedled and persisted. Eventually I sang it.

Supper. More food and more gifts. There was cold turkey and glistening ham. The various pickled delicacies included eggs, walnuts, cabbage and onions. There were tinned pears set in a strawberry jelly and cut-glass vases of celery gleamed by the cheese dishes. There was also the detestable carroway-seed cake. If forced to eat it, I'd pinch my nostrils before swallowing, for it was worse than any iron-based tonic to me.

In the middle of the table, however, stood the pièce de résistance. A cardboard galleon, covered in gold wrapping paper, had been constructed by Dorothy and Tom, my youngest aunt and uncle. It stood fully rigged with ropes that were really electric flex leading to fairy lights on the topsail. Replacing what might have been oars were scarlet streamers that ran from the hold towards every bread-plate round the table. As we hauled them in, these crêpe streamers brought us our final presents for the day.

Some time during that supper my own Christmas ended. My efforts to stay awake were the envy of all. I was anxious not to miss any further games. I excelled in organising teams and, when it came to riddles, I was a precocious horror who reeled off the answers before the questions had been completed. Yet, some time between ten and eleven o'clock, I still fell asleep in my mother's or grandmother's lap.

On Boxing Day the bars in *The Dolphin* reopened. I hardly glimpsed Aunt Maud and Uncle Ted. They were working non-stop, serving lunchtime crowds still boisterous with goodwill and an excess of food and drink. Cousin Norman cycled off to be with his own cousins and school friends of his own age. Even Aunt Marge understood that the clan gathering was over. With promises to write or visit within the first few weeks of the New Year, she made her way, old Grandma Marjoram trotting beside her, to the bus stop at the crossroads.

Within the following twelve months there was Munich. Early the next December my grandmother, for whose sake her children and her children-in-law forsook their own hearths each Christmas Day, died. None of us at *The Dolphin* could foresee such events. We couldn't guess that for us, as a family, there'd be no such Christmas again.

TO ST MARY'S

began, so I'm told, with my christening. My own first impression of the church is associated with the wedding of my father's sister, Aunt Dorothy. I was four: a page boy in blue cotton-velvet trousers and with a frilled shirt in a matching shade of satin. Sometime during the evenings that preceded that Saturday wedding I climbed onto a dining chair while my mother snipped here and pinned there, complaining as she did so of the expense that had been incurred to provide this outfit. My father glanced up occasionally from his evening paper but offered no counter-argument. My mother was not to be put off:

–If they could find money for three bridesmaids' frocks, you'd think they could have stumped up a shilling or two for the page boy.

My father sighed, lit a Players' Navy Cut and went into the garden to thin out the spring carrots and radishes.

As a page boy I looked well enough. I was never a handsome child. My mother told me that, yet she offered a crumb:

–You'll pass well enough in a crowd.

At the age of three and a half I'd developed a cast in my left eye. This did not right itself naturally until late adolescence and then – probably – as a result of the bewildering and delightful awareness that I was loved for the first time as a person. That was more than a dozen years into the future and hundreds of miles from the environment in which I was reared.

So, one month after my fourth birthday I set off: snub-nosed, mop-headed and wearing a pair of glasses, to carry my aunt's train as we processed along the aisle of Twickenham's parish church. It stands on the site of a fourteenth-century construction of which now only the tower remains. The body of the present church was built in the eighteenth century, at a time when the then riverside village was favoured as a rural retreat by the gentry. It wasn't too expensive, either, for those who worked in the arts.

As we made our way that afternoon between pews full of relatives in hired morning suits and home-made long frocks, I hardly glanced from side to side and certainly did not look down. Had I done so, I doubt whether I'd have been able to decipher the inscriptions on those tombstones set in the nave. Alexander Pope would have meant nothing to me. Nor was I aware that former worshippers included the Princesses Mary and Anne, daughters of James II. Of course, I had seen an imposing building next to the vicarage. I'd heard it referred to as York House but knew nothing of its history as a country home for James, Duke of York, and his daughters. And I was quite unaware that it had, during my infancy, become the town hall for the newly-created Borough of Twickenham.

Within a couple of years of that wedding day I became very well acquainted with St Mary's. Encouraged by my father, I worked on the rudiments of a sweet and clear treble voice. Unlike my brother, I'd no sense of true pitch. Without heavy prompting from an accompanist at the piano or organ I'd wander with blithe unconcern from key to key. The more this was pointed out, the more apprehensive I became. All to no avail. My father had been a choirboy at Portsea parish church years before when Cosmo Gordon Lang (later Archbishop of Canterbury, and equally famed for his pretty curates and his intrigues in the Abdication crisis) had been vicar there. Ergo, I was to be a choirboy at St Mary's.

At six I became a probationer, entitled to wear a black cassock and frilled collar but not a white surplice. Since I was, by then, attending a church rather than a state school, the basic hymns and psalms as well as the most familiar prayers and collects were well known to me. I learned them orally as I learned multiplication tables with scant reference to the texts. This can be the only explanation for an early confusion in my mind. One phrase in what is called the General Confession struck me as disturbing.

–Give us that Jew's sense of all Thy mercies. . .

It was oddly incompatible with a Protestant upbringing.

Sometime later, during an extra-tedious sermon, I flicked through the Book of Common Prayer and found:
–Give us that due sense of all Thy mercies. . .
Well before that I'd graduated to full choirboy. There were two practices a week: boys only on Thursday evenings and a full dress rehearsal of anthems with altos, tenors and basses on Fridays. On the Thursday that I was admitted as a full member of the choir I was tossed by the other boys high up into an enormous holly tree that overshadowed the churchyard. The resultant scratches on my face, hands and legs – a blooding among the berries – were evidence that I'd successfully withstood the initiation test.

I know I didn't cry. The experience wasn't pleasant but it was far less daunting than the rite to which boys were subjected when their voices broke and they had to abandon singing for a couple of years before returning – sometimes – as adults. When my turn came, I used my fists and feet to avoid the debagging and communal stimulation that took place in a shadowy corner of the churchyard well away from the gas lights in Ferry Lane. Smaller boys were shooed off to the chip shop so it was not until I was ten that I'd my first experience of touching pubic hair. Though Roger Smith's head was covered with soft carroty curls, his pubic patch was – to my fingers – as coarse as wire wool or the horsehair stuffing that fell in clumps from my grandmother's fireside chairs.

The Infants and Junior School that I attended being associated with St Mary's, some emphasis on a social conscience was to be expected. In addition to singing occasional mission hymns:

> *Over the sea there are little brown children,*
> *They have not heard of Jesus' name*

we were urged from time to time to bring contributions of various kinds to help worthwhile causes. I took my worn teddy bear and dog-eared story books so that the children of South Wales miners should have some toys to make their Christmas Day a little brighter: some glimmer in the diurnal poverty they experienced throughout that grim decade. Much more frequently I pestered my parents and any weekend visitors for farthings that might have lodged in the seams of their purses or pockets.

Monday morning at school was collection time. The project

was the new Church Hall. In each classroom we'd a large old-style sweet jar with a ground-glass stopper. How many jars had been filled with farthings before I became involved I can't hazard. The project seemed to stretch on and on into a limitless future, though it can hardly have continued much beyond my seventh birthday.

The building was finished at last: a splendid structure with a stage and dressing-room. The auditorium had a polished pine floor: anyone wearing hob-nailed boots had to remove them and walk in his socks. St Mary's Hall was ready for whist drives, music festivals and the annual productions of the Amateur Operatic Society. The old building a couple of hundred yards away could be abandoned to boy scout meetings or the occasional performance by ad hoc groups of unemployed actors who'd bring us potted versions of *Alice in Wonderland* or *Peter Pan*.

For the builders to have handed the keys of the new hall to the church verger would have been anticlimactic after all the door-to-door collections, the jumble sales and the benefit concerts that had been organised for the cause. A more public celebration was called for.

One Sunday morning in summer, the clergy and choir robed in the new hall. The building having been blessed, we processed across Church Street for Matins.

The Mayor was in attendance in scarlet trimmed with gold lace. The Town Clerk wore a white bob-wig, a throttling wing collar and Geneva bands. Aldermen were dressed in scarlet and the Councillors in blue. Many of these had been elected by my relatives and their friends. I knew them vaguely and nodded shyly. It's possible that there was the odd Liberal or even Labour infiltrator, representing the housing estates that were being constructed along our new arterial road. If there was, I wouldn't have known him.

Our focus that morning was not on our local dignitaries but on the diocesan Bishop of London: The Right Honourable and Right Reverend Dr. Arthur Foley Winnington Ingram. He was as august and distant as his name. Known to be a friend of Queen Mary, he would have met – as a young man – elderly clerics who'd have seen his predecessor at St Paul's still wearing a white wig (check any print of Victoria's coronation). Winnington Ingram was far more sumptuous in cope and

mitre of sapphire and gold with matching accessories: flashing
ring and gilt crozier.

Our new curate, clear-eyed and fresh-minted from St David's,
Lampeter, had been appointed chaplain to the bishop for the
service. We choirboys were in our places already when this
ill-matched pair approached the chancel. Our devout curate
sang the processional hymn with downcast gaze and finger-
tips extended in prayer. Winnington Ingram strode behind,
wielding his crozier and surveying the suburban congregation
with a metropolitan distaste.

It was as they neared the sanctuary that I first realised there
must be a way of doing things liturgically just as precise
as the rituals governing the changing of the guard outside
Buckingham Palace. Our curate, unaware that he should not
precede his superior into the sanctuary, walked on through
the open gates. Deft as an angler, Winnington Ingram flicked
his crozier and hooked it inside the curate's hood – an
unassuming little number edged with rabbit's fur. Choking
and scarlet-faced, the hapless youth stumbled and fell to one
knee while the bishop strode on alone. I saw the drama rather
than the comedy. The breathless curate reminded me of the
tale of Thomas à Becket stricken at the altar. I regretted that
there was no evidence of blood.

At Evensong we'd another episcopal visit but from a much
friendlier soul. Dr Bertram Simpson, Suffragan Bishop of
Kensington, arrived by the number 27 bus. He must, even then,
have seemed an anachronistic figure to fellow-passengers. To
my mind, his street gear would have been more suited to
one of the comic operas in which my Uncle Tom and Aunt
Dorothy took part. Dr Simpson's boots were black. So were
his gaiters, his frock coat and his top hat, with its rosette in
front and a couple of cords that linked the brim to the high
crown. Only a suspicion of purple at the throat distinguished
this bishop from the better type of undertaker. He carried an
ancient Gladstone bag which held his Do-It-Yourself kit: a
neatly folded set of vestments and a crozier that unscrewed.
Suffragans, I assumed, were not entitled to ostentation. His
crozier was a simple shepherd's crook of oak and brass.

The man had a merry face. His smile almost suggested a
wish to distance himself from the austerity of most of his
colleagues. He was the first senior cleric I'd seen who had

black rather than wispy grey hair. When the service was over I'd no hesitation in asking for his autograph. While writing in my album he apologised:

–Can't think why you should want this, you know. I'm nowhere near as famous as any of these Hollywood film stars. Mind you, I was taken for Harold Lloyd the other day. Someone asked me when he'd see me next at somewhere called the Odeon.

Laughter in the vestry or anywhere within the church precincts? It was a rare moment. Laughter, like the exuberance of childhood or the joy of a summer's morning, was something to be acknowledged with a fleeting smile and borne with fortitude by so many in that congregation. Soon, soon the autumn, the decay, special prayers for the dying and the Rememberance Day service in November. Christmas was a bit of a trial with all those tidings of joy. Nevertheless, even that joy could be moderated by references to the Magi's gifts including myrrh, foreshadowing death and a sepulchre.

Such a concentration on the proximity of death held no terrors for me. It was no more remarkable as a topic of conversation than the price of vegetables. I remember occasion after occasion when I'd stand with relatives by the banks at Twickenham Junction while they chatted with acquaintances:

–It's got him in the throat, my dear. It'll be a painful death. They'll give him morphia towards the end, of course. . .

–Don't care for the look of her at all, and that's a fact. She's got a pinched look round the nostrils, and we all know what that means. . . In certain lights you can spot that tell-tale tinge of yellow at the temples.

–Just opened him up, they did, and took one look. There was no point in bothering. Couldn't do a thing for him, they couldn't. Stitched him up again, they did, and sent him home to wait.

Small wonder that my first funeral – I was seven at the time – meant no more to me than singing *Lead, kindly light amid the encircling gloom* or *Abide with me, fast falls the eventide*. The only thing that dispelled the gathering darkness and the encircling gloom was the prospect of an extra sixpence at the end of the service.

So many corpses rested in the chancel in front of me at an impressionable age that I was never scared by ghost stories.

I noticed weeping among families in the congregation but I wasn't touched. There was too much of all that at home. I concentrated on the sixpence. It would go towards my holiday money or would buy another lead animal or a five-barred gate for my farmyard.

If I turned death to economic advantage, I was not the first in my family to do so.

As a London child in 1870 or thereabouts, Great-aunt Alice had worked out a nice little routine to raise the wind when she and her friends were short of pocket money. They hired themselves out as a corps of mutes. Having noted a house in front of which straw had been laid to muffle the crunch of carriage wheels on gravel, they'd bet – fairly safely – on an imminent death. A bit of delicacy and tact and they'd elicited the date of the funeral. Well before the cortège had moved off, they'd have slipped into little black numbers; every Victorian had one. And there they'd be, at the front gate of the relevant house, handkerchiefs at the ready. Having negotiated a fee with the chief mourner, they'd snuffle and wail their way behind the hearse to the nearest cemetery.

There were brighter moments at St Mary's. I must concede that. We did have weddings, too. But my fee was the same so, with equal dispassion, I'd sing *Love divine, all loves excelling* or *O perfect love*. Since the words were familiar, I was free to divide my interest between the younger bridesmaids – often classmates looking demure but uncomfortable in long frocks that demonstrated the impact of *Snow White* on local dressmakers – and the best man who would, now and again, take a nostalgic or speculative glance round the choir.

Weddings and funerals: these were the punctuation marks without which all the morning and evening services would blur now into one long dirge. Not that Matins and Evensong completed my Sunday duties. There was morning Sunday school at ten and afternoon Sunday school at three. I commuted endlessly between church and home. The visits of relatives offered no escape; nor did summer picnics by the Thames in Ham Fields. My father, checking his gold watch twice an hour, would remind me that I'd better change back from my swimming trunks or I'd miss the next ferry across to the Middlesex bank and be late for Evensong. I'd do so but I'd count the weeks until our next holiday in Portsmouth.

There was always the possibility of a guest preacher. Anything to relieve the tedium of our wheezing and lumbering vicar, the kindly but oh, so boring Reverend Prebendary W.P. Cole Sheane, Rural Dean of Hampton. Weeks before it happened, I'd anticipate a return visit by the chaplain for the Missions to Seamen. That was before I understood the older boys' jokes about emissions of seamen or semen.

When that chaplain stood in the pulpit I watched transfixed, quite certain that one evening he'd transmute into the knitting sheep in *Alice in Wonderland* he so much resembled. He looked like a sheep; he bleated like one. As a seven-year-old I'd every hope that he would produce two large wooden needles and a ball of pastel wool. Why shouldn't he, as he rambled on, knock up a bedjacket for my grandmother who often hinted that she'd like a new one for Christmas? If I could be thinking of other things while seeming to concentrate on his words then surely, I reasoned, so could he.

Just how early in my career as a choirboy I learned the trick of assuming an interest in the sermon while planning a joint adventure with my friend Alec who sat opposite me, I don't know. Alec and I were in the same class at school. In our spare time we were inseparable. His father owned a greasy spoon café not far from the station. On Saturdays and during school holidays he'd provide the pair of us with sandwiches and buns that would keep us going as we cycled away to explore what was left of the Middlesex villages.

Alec was not my archetypal copper-haired friend but he was the first in a succession of understudies. *The* copper-haired-friend to whom I was attracted instinctively and who was almost certainly unaware of my existence, crossed my landscape when I was six.

One autumn morning, in the care of a neighbouring twelve-year-old, I turned the corner from our avenue into the road that led past the girls' County School and on towards the station. Cycling towards us, emerging from a light mist, a thirteen-year-old boy rode with both hands in his trouser pockets on his way to Thames Valley School.

I saw him in profile as he passed; noted the jaunty angle of his maroon and green cap that had been pushed back and sideways to display his wavy copper hair. He was no frail and flaxen youth. His features were sturdy but not heavy. The nose was still boyish – the only thing about him untouched by puberty and self-awareness.

We saw him fairly regularly after that. As we approached he'd turn for a moment and we'd see him full-face. Undoubtedly his interest was in the twelve-year-old girl who was taking me to school. Even at six I realised that but it in no way deterred me from studying him. His eyelashes, darker than his hair, gave some extra firmness to his light blue eyes. And he'd another characteristic that I've found irresistible ever since: there was an almost translucent pinkness in his upper eyelids which gave them a sensuousness and dreamy vulnerability.

He was – and as a prototype still is – my childhood fellow-knight with whom I wished to ride: the compact body that complements my leaner frame, blue eyes to my brown, the fairer head that's laid against the dark. Alec was the first of his understudies. Of those who've followed, many have failed at the first tests: too wet; too egocentric or too involved elsewhere. As for the prototype, I learned only his first name: Dinky.

If Dinky excited me in a way to which I could put no name, it was Alex in whose company I was happiest. We'd swop cigarette cards and marbles and share our sweets. By the time we were nine we'd discuss anything unusual that we'd noticed during church services.

Maybe it was Alec who first mentioned the curious activities of older members of the choir during those evening sermons. I'd noticed for myself the odd mannerisms of one of our hooting altos. Yes, the man had almost the right coloured hair but it was rusty rather than copper. He'd little else to recommend him though, apart from what I at first took to be an unfortunate affliction. He appeared to have a tic similar to that which troubled a trombone-playing Salvationist who rehearsed hymns by an open window opposite my bedroom in the next avenue. The alto, unlike the Salvationist, suffered only temporary spasms, it seemed to me. After the sermon and later, when the service was over, there was no evidence of weird mannerisms as he chatted to his wife and children.

Why then did he persist, as the vicar droned on, in touching first his lips with one finger and then, seconds later, why should he stroke the left side of his nose so persistently? What explanation could there be for the way he'd tweak his lower eyelid? Since these gestures were made in no apparent order they had to be signals. This implied collusion with someone else and it couldn't be the man's wife for she stared fixedly at the pulpit.

By wriggling a little and risking a cuff on the ear from the baritone seated behind me, I managed to observe one of the younger tenors. During those intervals in which the alto ceased fingering himself, the tenor signalled a casual and silent reply. No more than a couple of Sundays later the tenor, who was himself a former choirboy, asked whether I would slip a note through the letter-box of a girl neighbour of ours on whom he was keen. With rare bravado I agreed to do so if he'd enlighten me about the mysterious sign language into which he'd obviously been initiated. He was reluctant but I had his letter in my pocket. He struck a hard bargain: one letter merited only one symbol. At least I learned that a gentle tapping of the nose with a forefinger signified a yen or hankering for. Not that I was any wiser as to what a yen might be. Nor am I any more certain – even now – of the origin of this covert method of communication or how prevalent it might be.

At much the same time, and again quite by chance, I noticed that there was another means of communication invisible to the congregation. Alec was as much at a loss to explain it as I was. The two senior choirboys on his side of the chancel would have been about thirteen. Between open chinks of the fretted choirstalls I watched one of them slide his hand into the pocket of his neighbour's cassock. I waited for it to be thumped silently. The movement seemed such a mean and stealthy way of robbing a fellow-chorister of his sweets or pocket money.

The victim did no such thing. He stared with a concentrated frown at the preacher but that, I knew, meant nothing. What could he really be thinking about so deeply that he didn't feel an intrusive hand in his pocket? He was, after all, a lively and intelligent lad, keen on diving and table tennis. I could only think that he was engrossed in dreaming about future contests. It wasn't a satisfactory explanation but Alec and I could think of no other.

Once a year – and in public too – we could communicate as loudly and as often as we wished. Not even the vicar's wife complained if we shouted and jumped and laughed. It was the choir treat. This summer outing was paid for from the Choir and Organ Fund for which there was an annual collection. How far we went depended on the weather: unpredictable then, now and always in England. For days we'd scan forecasts in the papers and listen to the wireless. As we wandered home from choir practice we'd ask men working late on their allotments for a weekend prediction: would a day trip on the Thames be feasible?

Most years it was although there was one dreadful July day that was ruined for us by storms and cloudbursts. Instead of making for London we had to be content with a visit to the Luxor cinema and tea in what had become known, by then, as the Parish Room. I still remember clearly the opening of H.G. Wells's *Things To Come* that we watched that Saturday afternoon: a fantasy of searchlights probing the Christmas skies, the subsequent war from which Ralph Richardson strode unscathed in a leopard's skin. To me it was all one with the weekly adventures I absorbed from my copy of *The Hotspur* and Alec's copy of *The Rover*.

Those trips on the Thames thrilled me equally but in a different way. I was off, if not to Treasure Island or to India, then at least to the estuary of the river. There I could taste salt on my lips and dream of mornings when I would be old enough to voyage on and on and be answerable to no one.

First, however, there was what seemed an interminable journey on the District Line of London's Underground to Mark Lane. Traces of the station can still be seen today just before the trains enter Tower Hill, further to the east.

Out of the compartments at last, we'd canter away – shouting and whistling – through a few cobbled streets that led to Tower Pier. And there she'd be waiting, spacious and imposing: *The Golden Eagle* or *The Golden Daffodil*. They were both part of a fleet of Thames paddle-steamers that plied daily to the river mouth and the Londoners' playgrounds of Margate and Clacton. They were to become – though none of us could have guessed – a couple of the little ships that would help to snatch some victory from the defeat of Dunkirk in 1940.

It seemed to me then that no more than five minutes passed between our boarding and departure. There were gangways to be climbed and slid down, a cafeteria to be sampled and landmarks to be recognised from the promenade deck. Across the oily waters of the Thames I could spot desolate wharves on the south bank that would have been familiar – even a hundred years later – to Oliver Twist, Nancy and Bill Sykes had they been able to escape from the margins of Dickens's fiction and assume an independence outside his imagination and ours.

Having cast off, we'd make quickly for the deeper channels of the Lower Thames. I'd learned from my father that the left side of any craft should be referred to as the port bow. So, soon enough, there'd be Wapping Old Stairs visible from our port bow. My mother had reminded me to look out for this grim landmark. She'd informed me with some relish that condemned criminals had once been sent there. They were suspended sufficiently low over the water for them to be immersed completely at high tide. After three tides they were deemed to be dead. Just another little picturesque anecdote to nourish a seven-year-old's imagination.

Not many minutes later, I'd move to the starboard side of the prow to watch Greenwich Palace in its opulent grounds shaping up through a mid-morning haze. The vicar toured among us, reminding each group that we were about to cross from west to east along the invisible line that marked zero degrees of longitude. It's very likely that I nodded, politeness having been dinned into me. I'm equally sure I would have been imagining poor Queen Anne Boleyn crossing the water by barge. She would have left her father's house, where West Ham Football Club grounds now stand, to meet King Henry in his palace and enjoy a fleeting happiness.

Past Tilbury and Gravesend the river widened so that, as we edged away from Southend Pier, the Isle of Sheppey appeared to be little more than a smudge on the southern horizon.

The paddles turned on and on, churning up water that became more sandy by the mile. The Thames mud was behind us. Becoming hungrier and hungrier, I lost all interest in the estuaries of the Rivers Crouch and Blackwater. I was the look-out at the prow, scanning ahead in search of a frail blur that would signify Clacton-on-Sea, packed lunches and an hour's liberty in the amusement arcades.

To suggest that I now recall anything of the return journey – other than a few splintered images – would be a pretence. I bought a packet of five cigarettes for my father at Clacton as a souvenir. I do remember that. For my mother I bought a peach. I'd observed early in life that peaches could be depended on to guarantee a brief pause in her litany of complaints about life, poverty, our relatives and me.

I treated myself to a dashing sombrero of black cardboard and crêpe paper trimmed with orange cord. This was worn throughout the homeward voyage until, as the paddles turned more sluggishly and we eased towards our moorings by the Tower, I let it drop back on my shoulders. Worn in this position, I hoped it would make me look as carelessly confident as Geronimo, the folk hero of a film that had impressed me.

Drowsy from the all-day journey and those few gulps of sea air, I was suddenly awake. Urged by fellow-passengers, I ran with them to the lower deck. We were being welcomed back to London by mudlarks.

A dozen of them, maybe more, formed an animated frieze as they dived around us under the lights along Tower Pier. Each one stretched his lips with his fingers before whistling to catch our attention. There was no more than a suggestion of individuality among them since each boy was covered, crown to toes, in wet river mud. A gallery of clay statues ready for firing in the kiln? That would be a fanciful and sentimental way of portraying them.

Mostly they dived. Those who couldn't, or were too young, leapt from the landing stage for which our boat was making. No sooner had they disappeared into the mud to retrieve our coins than they scrambled from it towards the steps again. Having deposited their winnings on a ledge, they were eager to forage once more deep into the sludgy bank of the Thames.

Grey as that mud they were, almost of it, except that they glistened and writhed, exuberant and unpredictable as tadpoles in the glare of the lamps. Only their eyes were undulled. Their glances raked the line of us as we leaned against the guardrails. Eye contact was brief. As they cajoled and whistled to us to flip them a penny, a ha'penny or even a farthing, we would have been no more individuals to them than they were to us. It was what we might give, not who we might be, that concerned them. Right they were, too. Just who were we

71

anyway, more than another boat-load of trippers? In five minutes we'd be gone, to be replaced by another batch on a craft that was already making its way, framed in lights, under Tower Bridge.

Why should I, young as I was, have thought of remaining among them? I did not envy the filth in which they worked or the patched and drooping undershorts that needed to be hauled up every other minute. I'd no horror of dirt and mud but, for me, there were other options if I needed to earn extra pocket money. Choirboy is a clean occupation and the weddings and funerals market, unlike the tourist trade, never slumps in winter. I think now that those coins for which the mudlarks plunged might have been more vital than spare cash for chips or cigarettes or a football. The poverty in London's East End did not ease until World War II. Those coins we threw might very well have been earmarked for tiny luxuries – even necessities – in some means-tested household by Whitechapel Market or off the Ratcliffe Highway.

For all that, I'd have been content to remain with them. Better that, I thought, than return to the hat and cap raising, carefully spoken, lace-curtained community in which we existed.

Around me on the deck the adults, and some choirboys, commented on the mudlarks' roughness of speech and a frequent expletive that was as muddy as their world. I stayed silent but I was certain already that such judgements were petty-minded. Those cockney boys had a vitality not brainwashed away by teachers such as my own, intent on producing model citizens. Nor had it been curbed by prim relatives whose watchword was decency – particularly as applied to the human body. While we were disembarking that night, some of the young divers were discarding their undershorts with a hoarse whoop. They were unashamed of their limbs that were about to shoot up into adolescence.

It was not their bodies that lured me but their vitality. Sure, I was a member of a gang at home. Yes, I went scrumping for unripe apples and plundered Twickenham's few remaining fields for rhubarb or strawberries. A bit squeamishly I even scrambled among branches in the parks for birds' eggs to add to my paltry collection.

Yet it was to that gang of cockney mudlarks I was drawn even though my accent would probably have precluded entry.

72

What was I looking for? Or whom? A livelier friend than Alec, perhaps? An older one, more worldly-wise, like Dinky with his copper curls? I neither knew nor cared whether any of the mudlarks was blond or black-haired under those grey clots of mud. The need that stirred in me was to share with someone the laughter I'd been taught to repress, together with any other disquieting symptoms of my dawning individuality.

Would any of them have reciprocated? Not that summer, I suspect. I'd have been a passenger among them. Since we didn't tolerate passengers in our gang there was no reason for me to suppose that the mudlarks would have done, either. Would I have been acceptable later, in summers to come?

I think I might have found among them more quickly than I did elsewhere that friendship for which I was dimly and dumbly searching. That's no whimsical notion. I've proved the easy and unanguished affection of London lads a dozen times. Having accepted them as themselves and trusted that they might accept me likewise, I've never been disappointed. Oddly, it's never occurred to me to ask any one of them whether he might have been one of those children – my own contemporaries – who risked filling his lungs with mud on summer evenings for a farthing.

TO THE OTHER LONDON

unless we were sight-seeing, would be to my mother's sister, Florrie. Whatever the reason, our visits to London involved a nineteen-minute journey by fast train to Waterloo. Sightseeing with my grandmother has now blurred to a scrapbook of images: ravens hopping over cobbles in some courtyard of the Tower, marvelling at the Whispering Gallery in St Paul's Cathedral and riding, high on an elephant's howdah, at Regent's Park Zoo. Wherever our destination, a descent into the Underground seemed to be necessary. Visits to Aunt Florrie, however, were with my parents when I was very young. She lived south of the Thames. To reach whichever flat she was living in at the time we'd either walk or take a tram.

She was the poorest of our family. What spare coppers she had were needed to support herself and her one surviving son. It was by her absence rather than her presence that I first began to distinguish her from my other relatives. She was, after all, the only one of us who lived in London, nearest to the scene of those national events to which we went as a family group. Yet she was never with us. As we pushed among crowds to glimpse coaches on their way to the weddings of the then Dukes of Gloucester and Kent, or shuffled along Millbank for half a morning before filing through Westminster Hall to gawp at the coffin of George V, Aunt Florrie was elsewhere, working.

Not until I was eight or maybe nine did I become aware that my aunt's was a single-parent household. When I asked after her husband I was told that he'd gone away. Since the answer was given without a sniff or a sigh, I thought it a pretty safe guess that he wasn't dead. That he was very much alive and living in South London I learned by accident. I happened to be with my aunt on her Saturday afternoon shopping tour of Brixton. We were crossing the entrance to Coldharbour Lane. I found the name puzzling:

–How can there be a harbour so far from the river? Why's it cold, anyway?

–Hush, boy. I'll tell you later. Just stop chattering a minute, will you?

I did so and we stood there in silence with her hand on my shoulder.

Loping away into the foggy distance was an elderly man in a fraying gaberdine raincoat. He was wearing a cap so he may have been bald or grey or both. In his right hand he carried a shopping-bag made of what we called leatherette. Whether it was patterned, as many of them were, in lozenges of light and dark brown, I've no recollection.

He didn't turn so, after we'd waited immobile for a couple of minutes, Aunt Florrie hissed at me:

–That's the Old Man. Quick now, boy, we're off back this way.

She really did hiss for her dentures were ill-fitting and there was no money for replacements. We turned and hurried silently into the market.

I forgot to ask about Coldharbour Lane so it was only recently I learned the name derives from Cool Arbour Lane which, with its eighteenth-century overtones, sounds almost comically pastoral in the context of urban Brixton. I suppose I didn't repeat my question that particular Saturday afternoon because my interest in local history had flagged. The Old Man was far more fascinating.

My aunt, however, refused to discuss him. She merely confirmed that he had been her husband. Only through questioning my mother could I begin to flesh out a person in my imagination.

Old Cobby – or so it seemed to my mother – was a vile creature. He'd never abused my aunt physically. Instead, he'd taken some delight in humiliating her and this, very rightly, she resented. Aunt Florrie had had an unfair share of humiliation early in life. Through some mischance during her birth at Queen Charlotte's Lying-In Hospital at Waterloo, she was slightly lame. As the first of four children, she'd suffered the thoughtless taunts of urchins along the Walworth Road until her two younger brothers had grown sufficiently to protect her with their tongues and fists.

She was never a willing victim and must have hoped, when she became an apprentice at fourteen and began to take home a little money to her widowed mother, that she had put degradation behind her.

One Saturday evening young Florrie, together with her fellow-apprentices, went to a dance hall not far from her mother's flat. Walworth was never the West End but, in 1898, a Saturday evening hop would have been a decently conducted occasion with a Master of Ceremonies calling the waltzes, The Lancers and a polka. Delighted to be making her way round the hall with a young man and in the company of her own friends at last, she became aware of some commotion at the door. Her mother – my maternal grandmother – crazed equally by Scottish Calvinism and a difficult menopause – was shoving couples aside and was about to tear across the floor.

–I'll have no daughter of mine seduced in this haunt of the Devil. Out of this now, my girl, and back to a Christian home. And back young Florrie was dragged – by her hair.

To Flora Finlayson from the Isle of Arran, dance halls were the prelude to perdition and theatres, so she alleged, a temptation to every imaginable vice. Her own behaviour wasn't quite as principled. She'd been twice to the Lyceum Theatre, just across Waterloo Bridge, to see Sir Henry Irving's performance in *The Bells* and enthused about it to her family. But then the Victorians' capacity for hypocrisy, more cunningly swathed than their sexual preoccupations and their mental sadism, can never be sufficiently underlined.

It was one afternoon in winter that I first began to understand just how far the major part of Aunt Florrie's life was a saga of tragedies. My mother sat preoccupied over a cup of tea in our living room. I'd been told to play quietly with my train set and not disturb her. Something unusual must have happened. I knew that, for my mother had just returned from the telephone to which she'd been called by a neighbour who lived opposite. Of the one hundred and twenty houses in Laurel Avenue, no more than half a dozen had phones.

To ordinary people such as ourselves, telephones were not for a daily gossip. They were not as ominous as telegrams, which presaged births, marriages and deaths. More likely a phone call would bring intimations of unsuspected developments: arrivals, or departures, or the onset of an illness. Day-to-day news came by letter: my mother would dash off four of five sheets as she waited for the potatoes to soften.

–Why on earth don't you write to them? You do seem to make such heavy weather about scribbling a few lines. If you write just as you speak, the rest will look after itself.

That was her invariable advice to my father. For him it was necessary, even when summarising family news for his brothers, to make a rough draft first. The whole business entailed a specially brewed pot of tea and three or four cigarettes. I kept out of the way for letter writing inevitably made him tetchy.

Whatever the phone message to my mother had been, it clearly worried her. I could see that. She was staring out of the window at our leafless apple trees. I knelt in silence on the carpet and continued to assemble my Hornby train set.

At last she spoke:

–Margery.

Within five minutes, warm in scarves and gloves, we were on our way to that same post office in which my grandfather had died. As we hurried along the Heath Road towards King Street, my mother – in another of her rare expansive moments – outlined to me why it was necessary to send a telegram:

–Walter has been accused of having sticky fingers.

So Aunt Florrie's phone call had nothing to do with sickness. Her son, my cousin Walter, was employed by the Royal Arsenal Co-operative Society. The Co-op was popular throughout inner and suburban London, not only with Labour voters, because it operated a dividend scheme. For every pound spent in the stores, or with the Co-op's milkman, so many pennies would be credited to the purchaser's account. My mother's number was 275710 at our local branch. All the shoes I ever had during childhood were made to last until quarter day when *the divi* was paid out in vouchers. We then trekked from the grocery department at Twickenham Junction to the clothes department across the Richmond Road.

Walter had been accused that Friday evening of fiddling the till. When the day's takings had been totted up there'd been a shortfall of twenty pounds. The charge was almost certainly unfounded. Sallow-skinned and uncertain twenty-year-old that he was, he would have been incapable of such an act even though it was known that he yearned for the deposit on a motor-bike – the South Londoner's pre-war Rolls Royce. It's likely the branch manager thought the lad innocent. He gave my cousin until the following Monday to replace the money – equivalent to twenty week's wages – or be sacked and then maybe prosecuted. Even had there been no legal consequences, Walter would have been dismissed without a reference. He would, in a phrase still current at the time, have lost his character.

An hour later and we were home again. Another hour and my mother was called to the phone a second time. Within minutes she returned, weeping. She was a woman who did not show gratitude comfortably. Yet she cried. Without being unjust, I feel she was aware that the circumstances demanded emotion. A novelettish situation had grown flesh and was among us. There was even a light fall of snow outside our window. Inside, warm by the open fire, my mother could rejoice that family tragedy and disgrace had been averted. It was one of our family's favourite tableaux: the shedding of good-hearted tears.

Aunt Marge, it seemed, had come to the rescue. No doubt she was gratified to be cast as a rescuing angel in a waft of heliotrope. She'd wired the money and Walter would be expected to repay her at five shillings a week from his salary for the following eighteen months.

He did. With the final installment he dispatched a food-hamper from the Co-op as interest on Aunt Marge's capital. There was of course a more subtle interest that could never be repaid. Aunt Marge had forged another link with our family – this time with people she'd met twice.

Walter's mishap was the nadir of the Cobby household's reverses. Things could only improve. Shortly afterwards, my aunt graduated from scrubbing floors and taking in washing from the shopkeepers along the Walworth Road. Instead of making straight for Guinness's Buildings if we went to visit her during the week, we'd arrange to meet her from work in the West End. After shopping in Debenhams at sales time, my mother and I would take a bus from Kensington High Street – probably the 7 – and make for Oxford Street.

My mother, affecting to be more hopeless than she was on

geography, would rely on me to see that we alighted not too far from Marble Arch. We'd then cut through side streets to the superior antiques shop where my aunt worked as a cleaner and tea lady.

I am not a rich man so I must be prudent because the British libel laws are savage. Best not to specify the shop but its patrons then – maybe now – included many coroneted heads. After a heavy and liquid lunch, an uncle of Queen Elizabeth II had been known to lie on the floor there, drumming his fists and heels and screaming for his wife.

As my father said of the place:

–Even the darned proprietor's got a handle to her name.

We waited for my aunt across a narrow, foggy street. At half past five she'd emerge from the imposing doorway of the shop opposite. I was consumed with excitement for I'd heard, many times, one of her tales about that shop and there it was: Bluebeard's Castle with a secret I'd been dared to repeat.

Aunt Florrie could move freely around the many ground, first and second floor showrooms. This was obviously necessary since her working day consisted, for the most part, of waxing, polishing and dusting the choice exhibits. Although items were unpriced, they were always tagged with both the date and place of origin. Most were English or French and of the seventeenth, eighteenth or nineteenth centuries. Nothing made later than 1830 was stocked. There were smaller pieces of porcelain also, such as snuff-boxes. These had to be counted each morning. Occasionally, and at short notice, my aunt would be instructed to remove as many of these knick-knacks as her apron pockets would hold. The car of an eminently recognisable but light-fingered client had drawn up unexpectedly.

One stipulation had been enjoined on Aunt Florrie when she'd been engaged: she must never, ever, attempt to do more than dust some stairs that led to a flat roof on the top of the building.

Some months later, when she'd proved herself trustworthy, she was left alone one lunch-time. The proprietor had gone to keep a social engagement and the show-room staff were doing their Christmas shopping. My aunt, who lived in a tough area and walked to it nightly via unlit Hungerford Bridge, was not to be daunted by a few stairs that led to who could say what secrets.

Locking the street door from the inside, she hobbled away to the very top of those stairs, arming herself with a broomstick. It would serve, she thought, as part of an alibi if the owner returned: no one could be reprimanded for taking action against suspected burglars.

The door to the roof was not locked. There were no skeletons in cupboards. They were littered instead around the mossy concrete, protected from neighbours' curiosity by a high parapet. In the filth of a smoggy December day stood Georgian chairs reproduced faultlessly and only recently delivered from some country joinery. Not one but three William and Mary sideboards had been pushed into a corner where they were weathering nicely in the soot and rain. And there they'd stay, as Aunt Florrie realised, until the spring. Hosed down in the quiet of a Sunday morning, then hand-polished until they gleamed in the lights of a show-room, they'd be sold at top prices to the nouveau riche and the unsuspecting who, as my mother was quick to say, are always with us.

It was my secret hope, as I stamped my feet and waited on the damp pavement, that there'd be news of some fresh scandal. But no – all we got was a bleak smile and a wave as she limped towards us across the street. The shortest of her brothers and sisters, she'd their characteristic black hair and the full and expressive eyes. There was never any colour in her cheeks, summer or winter, for she'd the liverish complexion of many Londoners then – something that only she had inherited from an unknown grandfather.

We'd mingle with the home-going workers, crossing Piccadilly and skirting Trafalgar Square through the quieter streets. There was still the need to economise and my aunt, like my mother, never frittered money on unnecessary fares.

Sometime during those few minutes it took us to cut down from the Strand towards the old Charing Cross Underground station by the Embankment, my aunt would say it. I'd be waiting for the phrase she never failed to use:

–Never speak to a soul here, boy, whether it's moonshine or noon. The wickedest street in London, this is.

We'd be walking through Villiers Street at the time. What explanation she gave my mother for this remark I'll never know. I liked puzzles so, before I'd left Junior School, I'd made the connection between Villiers Street, Buckingham Street and Of Alley. They had been part of an estate given to George Villiers, Duke of Buckingham, by James I. History books borrowed from our local library informed me that this young Scottish nobleman was known affectionately by the king as Steenie. I concluded that he must have done something special and important for his monarch. Much later I discovered this to be true, in a rather private sense.

Even then, as we hurried towards Hungerford Bridge, I noticed a couple of other things. A number of unattached men seemed to linger in the shadowy doorways of the closed shops hoping that some passer-by would give them a light. It was never a married couple who paused to do so. And the strange little street named Of Alley always seemed to be as busy as Villiers Street itself. Again, it was single men who seemed to come and go. There was nothing in Of Alley other than a public loo. Having wondered what might be so fascinating about that, I improvised an urgent need to use it. Aunt Florrie's response was swift and emphatic:

–Then you'll just have to wait, boy. There's one by the station far cleaner than that filthy hole.

Having skipped along the boards of Hungerford Bridge through which the waters of the Thames twinkled in the darkness, I'd be hurried through the mean streets that surrounded Waterloo. Here, too, on the site of the South Bank arts complex, my aunt would insist that I hold her hand:

–Pay no attention to what's going on around you, boy.

Had she told me that the men and women chatting nervously on every corner were commuters and local prostitutes, or that the newsagents' windows were covered with unusual advertisements, I'd have been none the wiser.

So on we'd trudge, past the Old Vic Theatre, then the Elephant and Castle, reaching at last the tenement block in which Aunt Florrie rented two rooms on the third floor. To my mother, that grim block was an embodiment of the fate to which any of us might succumb through drink, non-payment of rent or unemployment. How could I, barely out of Infants' School, have had the wit to ask if such accommodation seemed so dreadful to those hundreds who lived there? Had those inner-city unskilled workers who first moved in during 1880 or thereabouts been ousted from gracious Regency terraces? More likely they'd come from shanties and courtyards so vile that the charity dwellings were a welcome alternative. Guinness's Buildings were at least dry, heatable, sanitary and not infested with rats.

The snugness of living in two rooms enthralled me. The food was prepared, eaten and digested in a space that – when my mother and I had left for home – would serve as a makeshift bedroom for my adult cousin. Beyond a bedspread that had been tacked to a length of string and hooked across a doorway there was my aunt's small bedroom. On arrival, we threw our coats and scarves on a double bed round which we had to edge our way.

The two women would chatter away as they prepared our meal. My cousin Walter would be thumbing silently through *Exchange and Mart* and I'd sit watching him, trying from time to time to think myself into his upbringing in that confined space. The room in which we sat had not been just for living and sleeping. It had been his world. Though he never voiced his detestation, I could see for myself the mechanical way in which he did everything that was asked of him. His focus was elsewhere and I guessed that he hated The Buildings as they were known. His determination to own a motor-bike was as understandable to me as my own dream of owning a horse and cantering away into the morning.

To Walter, that room may well have remained no more than an enlarged cot. Just as soon as he could be left – a little after he was twelve months old – he'd been tied around the waist with a rope. This, attached to a leg of the kitchen table, kept him at a safe distance from the fireguard. He was left, surrounded by a pillow, a bowl of food and a couple of toys. His mother then went off to scrub floors. That part of the day's work over, she'd return to Guinness's Buildings with sufficient filthy washing to keep her busy late into the evening, after a quick visit to buy food as the shops and markets were closing.

All that had passed when my aunt began work at the antiques shop. Yet the wallpaper was still impregnated with the sad odour of drying linen that had once hung overnight from ropes and pulleys round the ceiling. All the rinsing and boiling had been done outside Aunt Florrie's rooms and across the landing. On each floor there was a communal washroom with mangles for wringing out the clothes. Often, as I waited to use the communal loo, I'd wander into those grey cavernous washrooms. The harsh smell of soap and the disinfectant with which the floors had been sluiced is unforgettable.

Very slowly, this hand-to-mouth existence gave place to a way of life. Walter, soon after his debt to Aunt Marge was repaid, had a promotion. My aunt's own wages were raised. My father, congratulating her, added:

–Take the money. Don't bother your head about that. There's a darn fool born every minute. If one doesn't buy those fakes, another will. If we had your boss's gift of the gab we'd all be riding in Rolls Royces.

She took the money and moved from The Buildings at last. It was goodbye to Walworth. Aunt Florrie found a flat near Kennington Park where she'd once wheeled her children in a pram on Sunday afternoons. And there she stayed, in Traherne Road, until – like her neighbours – she was bombed out in the blitz of 1940. The whole road has now disappeared under a council estate.

In her new flat she'd the comparative luxury of a kitchen-cum-dining room, a front sitting room with windows that overlooked trees, a couple of bedrooms and a bathroom. So extensive must this have seemed to my cousin that he installed a private telephone to allow my aunt to call him whenever a meal was ready.

The table became more colourful with his purchases, at staff rates, from the Co-op. There'd be Elizabeth Lazenby's or John West's tinned salmon. My mother was quick to point out to her sister that the red variety was superior to the pink. There'd be Libby's tinned fruit salad served with Ideal Milk. The meal always ended with a Lyons' French Cream Sandwich. I looked forward to that despite its dusting of sugar so fine that I was reminded of face powder.

If my parents were with me for Saturday tea at Traherne Road, I'd soon be bored by the adults' conversation afterwards round the sitting room gasfire. The room was light and airy enough but it was lifeless. Upturning a madonna in a glass bottle so that snowflakes drifted around her china feet didn't grab my attention for long. Nor did the inevitable scraps of royal scandals that were recounted in disbelieving undertones. All I knew of the abdication of Edward VIII was the schoolboys' popular variant on a Christmas carol:

    Hark, the herald angels sing
    Mrs Simpson's pinched our king. . .

Some time during the evening my aunt could be relied on to relate what seemed to me a meaningless incident concerning an operating theatre. My experience of hospitals was slim but terrifying. Soon after my fifth birthday I'd had my tonsils yanked out.

Aunt Florrie's experience appeared to be somewhat different. In a sibilant whisper she'd imitate a chorus of voices that once surrounded her, encouraging her to push down and down, relax a moment and then push down one last time. It all seemed very odd to me as I listened from the other end of the room, pretending my attention was elsewhere.

I was meant to be improving my education. There were few books in the flat but I was always offered one particular cloth-bound volume. This contained the most horrendous collection of sepia and white photographs of troops at the Western Front in World War I. The effects of chlorine and gangrene on men, the studies of exploding horses and decomposing heads, I'd seen them all and dreamed them, too, well before my ninth birthday. At least it inured me, years later, to sights I saw daily as a reporter in Central Africa's Katanga war. As a child I accepted it as no more than another of the barbarities on which my mother's imagination tended to linger.

At Aunt Florrie's I could close that book. At home I'd be forced to listen to my mother as she read to me – over and over – the incident in Black Beauty in which a horse was maltreated. To be fair, she'd put the book aside once she'd succeeded in having me run screaming from the room. On holiday from Infants' School, I would be treated to extracts from her copy of *The Daily Telegraph and Morning Post*. There was a colourful description of the flogging of prisoners with the cat o' nine tails while some unspeakable chaplain counted potatoes into a pail to log the number of stripes. My mother's enthusiasm as she read this to me was equalled only by the zest with which she sang Scottish metrical versions of the Psalms as she prepared our lunch.

One theme in Aunt Florrie's conversation faded somewhere

along the way after she'd moved from Walworth to Kennington. There were no further references to her husband, Old Cobby, who'd stubbornly refused to wear a collar and tie because his wife's posh relatives were coming for tea. That appeared to me, even as a child, to be the oddest of reasons for two people to split up. I learned the awful truth much later. It wasn't drink. The man downed no more pints a week than many hard workers of his generation. Nor had he been unfaithful. The truth was whispered to me: Old Cobby had been a very early member of the British Communist Party. Since Aunt Florrie was never more than a token and unthinking Conservative, I'd guess it would have been pressure from her relatives – her sniffy Scottish aunts – that pushed her into leaving him.

Soon after my ninth birthday, I was deemed responsible enough to travel from home to Waterloo by myself, provided I was seated in the rear compartment of the train and one of my parents had spoken to the guard about me. At Waterloo, I'd be met by Aunt Florrie and could look forward to a weekend away from home. There was a recognition of my dawning individuality by my parents and relatives. I found it quite astounding that Aunt Florrie and my cousin had, prior to my arrival, discussed treats arranged especially for me.

Loaded with shopping bags, my aunt and I would take a tram along the Kennington Road. Whether we sat downstairs or had to stand in the aisle, I would stare up fascinated by those great terraced houses that rose higher than any I'd ever seen.

–The music hall stars used to live here. Now you see these side-streets, boy? There, down there, eh? That's where the chorus girls and boys used to have their digs.

Property would have been much cheaper then on the unfashionable side of the river and Kennington, with its frequent trams and its stables for hansom cabs, would have offered dependable transport to the many West End theatres.

There was one particular house for which I waited. Having pointed to it once, there was really no need for my aunt to remind me that, as we neared Kennington Cross, we'd pass the reputed but unmarked birthplace of my Saturday morning hero, Charlie Chaplin. Not Saturday mornings at Aunt Florrie's flat. I mean Saturdays in Twickenham where I'd be allowed to go to a children's matinee at one of the cinemas, if I could wheedle the sixpence out of my father.

If I was unsuccessful, it would be likely that I'd go with him anyway in the afternoon to the old Luxor in the Heath Road. My father enjoyed the live entertainment that was presented between the second feature film and the star attraction of the week. Entertainment on that shallow stage consisted of short turns by ageing music hall performers who were glad to be offered work even in a suburban cinema. I watched Nellie Wallace twirling her cobra-length feather boa, listened to Harry Champion as he gasped and wheezed his way through *Any Ol' Iron*, the one song that had been his trademark for years, and I tried to understand the jokes of George Robey, who'd soon have my father weeping with laughter but who my mother dismissed as a smutty red-nosed comedian.

Those were my Saturday afternoons in the suburbs. When I was at Aunt Florrie's, I knew better than to ask whether we might be going to the cinema. Of course I guessed we would but it had to be a surprise, so I got ready to look eager and delighted later in the day.

First there was the weekend shopping to be unpacked. As I helped with this we'd listen to the wireless. To Aunt Florrie, her bakelite-covered set was more vital than it would have been to any of my other relatives. They'd more money and wider choices of entertainment. Aunt Florrie listened to everything from Henry Hall and his orchestra to Uncle Mac on Children's Hour. Though she'd only a window-box she listened to the gardening programmes. Her wireless opened up a landscape beyond her four walls and it cost her less than a theatre ticket or a daily newspaper.

Tea over, we'd set off for the Trocadero cinema at the Elephant and Castle. There was never any discussion about the choice of cinema: the main film was a secondary consideration. To my aunt, my cousin and I, the Trocadero was – for different reasons – a dream palace. It was vast. Once inside, a trek in search of sweets or the loo gave me, I thought, basic training as an explorer. All other cinemas in South London were piddling compared with it. As for the Luxor at home, well, maybe it wasn't a flea-pit but it could never be more than a suburban apology.

The second feature film over, Cousin Walter would hurry off

to queue for ice creams. These we'd eat in a leisurely way during the Movietone News and some short clips from coming attractions. Then there was a second interval which seemed interminable to me. My impatience concealed excitement. I knew what was coming and the anticipation was comparable only to that I experienced at theatres during the overture.

Yes, the organ did rise from a pit and the organist was drenched in light from rainbow spots. Moments later the ruched tab curtains slid up noiselessly to reveal a full chorus. Girls in crinolines twirled flimsy parasols as they flirted silently with lads in sequinned top hats. These beaux wore white tail-coats and trousers and rested their white-gloved hands on silver walking-sticks.

And then they sang. What would it have been? *Songs From The Shows* would have been the generic title. I knew some of the tunes. The branch of our family that was much involved in amateur operatics sang them. There would have been selections from *Lilac Time* and *Show Boat* and, almost certainly, something by Franz Lehár. Aunt Florrie would hum the melodies. Walter and I would watch as we finished our choc ices. It seemed almost a private performance for us as the chorus waltzed or tap-danced on and on. Put another way, it was for all three of us a trip to a cosmos very far from the everyday. Things were becoming rosier in Traherne Road.

Next morning I'd repack my case. Not that I was being taken home directly. There was to be a further treat of a different kind. Walter had added a sidecar to his motor-bike. Another portent of a belated spring for the Cobby family.

Swathed in scarves I'd ride pillion. My aunt would heave herself into the sidecar, protecting herself from the weather in a leather coat and a leather helmet with ear-flaps. We'd speed through Clapham and Tooting then away into Surrey for a picnic lunch at Box Hill or on Ranmore Common.

A year or so later, when the extra furniture for the new flat had been paid for, we'd venture to the coast: Eastbourne or Hastings or Bexhill. There'd even be money for a toffee-apple or some of the spun candyfloss that stuck to my cheek like pink whiskers. There was never enough though for the funfair or a meal in a restaurant. Who cared? We all enjoyed paddling in the Channel: it was fun and cost nothing. For an hour or so my aunt and my cousin were children again with me. Years older than my mother, Aunt Florrie could unbend in a way my mother never managed to do.

Like me, my aunt welcomed the wind that cut our faces as we sped through the lanes, approaching roadside farms and smallholdings at such a speed that it seemed, until the last moment, that we must split them. I knew then I was glimpsing the landscape as it must have appeared to Donald Campbell in his *Blue Bird*.

It was during these expeditions that I noticed my aunt laughing for the first time. Each time I glanced down at that mini-submarine of a sidecar she'd turn, wave to me, and grin. At the time I didn't think of it as more than simple enjoyment. It never occured to me that she was into her sixties before she'd green hillsides to look at instead of the sour holly-green of washroom tiles. With one foot on the threshold of old age, she breathed the sharp air of the English Channel rather than the steam that rose from water fouled by other people's dirty clothes.

Late on Sunday afternoon I'd be taken home. Walter and Aunt Florrie would pause for tea with my parents before driving on to Kennington. There were weekends, and they became more frequent, when I'd have as soon hopped back on that pillion again and gone with them through streets of grey houses and dusty privet hedges to their flat which stood no more than five minutes' walk from where I'm now typing.

TO THE AMATEUR OPERATIC SOCIETY

Twickenham Operatic Society concentrated its enthusiasm – rather more than similar groups in nearby Richmond or Hounslow – on an annual production of one of Gilbert and Sullivan's nineteenth-century operettas. They made occasional excursions into the work of other composers but they were never very adventurous. The charming and sedative lyrics of Edward German, for instance, provided them with a safe alternative. His *Merrie England*, with its chorus of laundered and euphoric peasants, confirmed for me as a six-year-old that my illustrated history books were right. The past smelled sweeter than the present. I could make no connection between those well-shod and healthy villagers on stage and the inhabitants of Twickenham's back streets. Not a trace of snot or mud on stage: plenty on the kids with whom I roamed the fields and back alleys.

I wonder whether the performers ever questioned the accuracy of the landscape offered in *Merrie England* by Sir Edward's music or Basil Hood's libretto? It's doubtful. Far more pertinently to them, the show was stuffed with untaxing and melodic arias for all the leading singers. They were useful arias as well, since *O peaceful England* and *The yeomen of England* could always be revived less publicly after the Saturday night curtain had come down. What better for a bravura performance at the piano on Sunday evenings in the months that followed – even during the war years that were waiting, unsuspected, in the wings?

There was also German's *Tom Jones*, a sort of deodorised version of Fielding's novel. This was never as popular. True enough it had a waltz song, and the dances always formed a pleasing background to a garden party. As a show, however, it hadn't half the quotability of *Merrie England*. There was nothing in it that could match the rhetoric of *Where are the yeoman, the yeomen of England?* Having heard my father's rendering of that many times, I began to suspect that the said yeomen were alive and well in the nicer parts of Twickenham. Who could they be other than the teachers, clerical workers and businessmen? Once a year, rather like Father Christmas or the mayor at his inauguration, these stalwarts would don historical fancy dress to reaffirm their roles in the community.

The sentiments implicit in German's operettas suited Twickenham well at the time. It underlined an unquestioning and Conservative patriotism. Such sentiments were reinforced for me during my first experience of community singing.

Some months before I was enrolled at the local Infants' School, I was taken there one late May morning by my mother on what I suppose was a familiarisation visit. I stood on a chair in a great cavern of a classroom. With bewilderment I listened to the Mixed Infants, their teachers and our local vicar as they sang *What is the meaning of Empire Day?* Small Union Jacks were flourished throughout the performance but, alas, I don't recall one word of the lines that followed. By the time that I was ready to demand an answer to the big question posed in that opening line, such celebrations had been abandoned: the Empire had become a Commonwealth.

Since education was compulsory and Empire Day built into the timetable, there was no difficulty in recruiting that chorus. Twickenham Operatic Society, however, could hardly conscript members. The chorus was a perennial headache.

Of course there was always a dependable core of talented enthusiasts. How far this was an asset, how far a liability, was at times debatable. Gilbert and Sullivan, writing as they did for a company of whose abilities they were well aware, felt no need, when mapping out a new work, to employ every performer who'd happened to have starred in their last success. But that was the Savoy Opera Company, not Twickenham's amateurs. How could the resident contralto be placated if there was little more than a walk-on available in the next show? Should she be placated anyway? It was a problem for the contralto, too. Throwing a tantrum and walking out until a suitable role cropped up some time in the future might be construed as disloyalty to the group. More likely, she'd stomach the set-back, step aside gracefully into the chorus line and make sure she was well down-stage in ensembles. There were subtler indignities to be endured. The private dressing-room had to be abandoned and she'd have to scrummage with the rest for a chair and a hanger under the stage. There was the chance, however, of a little balm. It would often happen that some other nearby group might have a suitable part available in another show. Then the contralto, or the baritone or mezzo, could feel almost professional: two productions on the go at one time, even though complicated cross-county jaunts might be entailed.

A second problem, one commonly experienced by straight drama groups as well, was a dearth of young adult males. The sons and nephews of members with ears sufficiently true to croak a melody were coralled a week or so before any production. They'd a distressing tendency to defect immediately after the last night. Weekly rehearsals on late summer evenings were not for them. They preferred, understandably, to stroll with a girlfriend by the Thames, or go with their mates to a riverside pub.

Partly as a result of this dearth of male singers my youngest aunt and uncle gained an easy entrée into Twickenham's musical circles. Even had Dorothy not been married she would have been acceptable. She'd a pleasing mezzo voice and, for the most part, she had charm. Like me, she could be tempestuous under stress but, again like me, it was never more than a brief summer storm.

Her marriage to my Uncle Tom made her doubly welcome in the cheerless school halls where the shows were rehearsed. Tom had the dashing looks of a young rugby player, an easy social manner and, with training, a competent baritone voice. What he lacked initially in vocal technique was remedied quickly, for Dorothy was an able pianist and had an eye and ear for dramatic possibilities.

I can't have been more than five years old when I was taken, by my grandmother, to the dress rehearsal of the first show in which my aunt and uncle took part. Both were serving a year's apprenticeship in the chorus, without which it was impossible to audition for star status. I can't say where this particular production was staged. The acting area was so huddled that the chorus masked one another during ensembles, so it can't have been at York House, and St Mary's Hall hadn't then been built.

The title of the piece, *The Mermaid*, entranced me. I'd every hope that it might be a musical version of H.C. Andersen's fairy tale with which I was very familiar. It was no such thing but I was still excited as we waited for the entrance of the heroine. How would she be dressed – or undressed? Would the actress appear semi-nude, her breasts as bare as those of the statues in our Town Hall gardens? I've no idea of the way in which Messrs Simmonds or Fox of Covent Garden contrived a respectable costume. All that remains is a hazy recollection of a waist-length wig and an abundance of fish-net in which the mermaid had been caught. I've never seen an advertisement for any revival of this show. Were I to do so, I'd not waste an evening on it.

Throughout those years during which I learned to spell Abyssinia, Abdication and Czechoslovakia from the headlines of London's evening papers, the operatic society was offering its members more than just a chance to display their talents in public for a week. It provided them with a framework for their leisure, marking out the seasons for them as surely as an academic or ecclesiastical calendar might have done. Lads conscripted into the chorus came and went but those who formed the core of the group kept in touch, despite their small vendettas, after the final curtain-calls had been taken.

There were weekend rambles in the spring and summer months, and picnics in the Surrey countryside. I was too young to be taken on any of these but I savoured the names of the places visited: Newlands Corner where bluebells were gathered by the armful, or Box Hill, surrounded by a few remaining smallholdings from which honeycomb and eggs warm from the nest would be brought home.

Each summer, one of the more affluent members of the Society would give a garden party. Dart boards and a hoopla stall were set out among the rockeries and flower beds. Friends and relatives were invited so, one year, I won a tin of fifty Players' Navy Cut in the treasure hunt. My father took the cigarettes and I was given half a crown in compensation. When the flat navy-blue tin with its portrait of a bearded sailor stamped on the lid was empty, my mother kept it for her needles and cotton reels. It still serves the same purpose in my kitchen drawer.

Late in the afternoon, when a breeze got up or when the first soft patter of rain started to blur the lettering above the improvised stalls, everyone moved inside to a vast sitting room. There were those who secretly welcomed the wind and rain. It was an obvious excuse for the concert to begin early.

The items the performers chose were probably clues to their private aspirations. It was at such a concert that I first heard the Habañera from Bizet's *Carmen*. No doubt the performance was prettified by suburban respectability but the impact of those flashing and unpredictable chords and glissandi on me has remained. Yes, it was light-years from the flicks of Toledo steel that a singer such as Victoria de los Angeles could evoke. That conceded, the Society's second mezzo-soprano still used her chance to impress us all with a talent that should – in future – be offered more than the third of the Three Little Maids in Sullivan's *The Mikado*. She couldn't have hoped for much more: there was no likelihood of Bizet's opera being attempted. The group knew its limitations. Bizet, Lehár and Offenbach were for the two or three amateur grand opera companies that lingered in the nicer suburbs.

The garden party concert allowed other unsuspected talents to surface. The Society's resident tenor, a teacher in a local junior school, could demonstrate a comic gift that really wasn't demanded of him when playing Nanki Pooh, or Marco in *The Gondoliers*. He'd a penchant for monologues: a strange and dying art form that, like elocution, lasted until wartime radio with Jack Warner's droll recitations. Not that I recall one syllable of the tenor's repertoire.

What does remain is the mood of interested and polite amusement among the onlookers. Whatever their ages – twenty-six or sixty-six – they grouped themselves around the walls on chairs, or stood in huddles, or sat with me, cross-legged and child-like on the exotic carpets that were strewn around gleaming parquet floors. It was all very like the musical evenings at Aunt Marge's but on a more formal basis: part of an ancient legacy of self-entertainment that adapts to social conditions. No more than fifty years earlier, the forebears of those Twickenham entertainers, though factory or field-bound, would have been performing more

93

traditional songs learned by rote. But it was the thirties and the new lower-middle classes had won shorter working hours and were enjoying a toe-hold on respectability. They'd forgotten the folk-songs and country dances. Participation in a Gilbert and Sullivan operetta had taken their place for Sullivan's music was hummable and Gilbert's satire was safely reactionary.

Some time during the late summer each year a shadowy and mysterious body called the Committee would convene. It was for them to decide which operetta would be performed late in the following January or early in February. The Committee certainly included The Producer and The Conductor: neither could be mentioned in other than those hushed toned usually reserved for The Medical Specialist.

The Committee was composed of very human beings. There were tussles and arguments grounded in unstated motives; no doubt of that. The next production agreed and announced, the rumours seeped out. Dorothy was quick on the trail:

–It's as plain as the nose on your face, my dear. *She'd* have stopped at nothing to get a fat part for that pimply clerk she's carrying on with. Well, they've made their choice. Let's just see what sort of a fist that young man makes of the baritone lead.

There were darker hints, too, voiced by some of Dorothy's friends:

–D'you think what's-his-name's really up to doing those patter songs? I mean, what experience has he had? Now then, keep the party clean, I wasn't referring to unmentionable experiences. I'm sure his friendship with Mr Smallpiece is as pure as the driven slush. . .

Whatever the decisions and the motives underlying them, they imposed no great demand on The Conductor. He was an able musician who, in another context as organist and choirmaster, was happy to tackle a Bach or Haydn oratorio as a welcome holiday from the gloomy predictability of works by that most Victorian of trios, Stainer, Winn and Walker.

For the Twickenham Operatic Society there was an additional advantage in keeping to Gilbert and Sullivan. In a London theatre, and no more than half an hour away, the professional D'Oyly Carte company performed more or less the whole canon during the course of a couple of years. Performed is maybe too weak a verb: they enacted each light opera with a ritualistic devotion reminiscent of High Mass.

Twickenham's local amateurs didn't aim to replicate professional productions in our local halls. Well, not entirely. In one sense they had to. Any group throughout Britain that essayed a G&S operetta (as it was known backstage) had to conform to the traditional interpretation, stage business and musical tempi that had been established back in the eighteen eighties when the composer and librettist had been on speaking terms.

The only comparison that comes to mind is the inherited oral tradition of poems and sagas before the printed word. Even that is inexact. Scholars now accept that variants suited to local conditions, as well as changes that developed from the faulty memories of drunken or aged singers became admissible.

Not so with Gilbert and Sullivan. Each flick of the fan or toss of the peruke had to be learned. For only one musical number per opera was an encore permitted. Even the scenery could not be varied. When it arrived at the hall from Messrs Cape of Chiswick it might be a bit battered and show evidence of a recent touch-up. It would, nevertheless, be such a faithful replica of the original nineteenth-century set that the ghosts of William Schwenck Gilbert or Arthur Sullivan would have needed only one glance from the back of the hall before muttering *Ruddigore* or *Patience*. Not a chance that they might have been wrong.

But what if the principal actors or The Producer had been innovative? Suppose that there had been an attempt to update the ageing jokes and tiring stage business sometimes during those Tuesday to Saturday runs? It would have been hazardous. Copyright was held by the D'Oyly Carte family and they were reputed to send spies to rove through chapel halls and civic theatres across the land. It was pretty well certain that these custodians of the true faith paid at the door and then sat incognito at the back making notes of any heresies that might be perpetrated. Permission for future productions could be withheld.

It is to them that we were indebted for the ritualism that characterised the three little maids trio in *The Mikado*. So predictably stylised did it become that, by the time I was a student, post-war revues were sending it up. The mood had changed. To audiences in the fifties the spectacle of three women checking that they were exactly centre stage before opening their mouths was hilarious. So too was that anticipated moment when the women, far from being all contrary, knew it was more than their contracts were worth to do anything other than turn in unison, lift their left knees as though cycling and rotate their closed fans to the beat of the melody.

Only after the copyrights lapsed could Sullivan be used as background music to television commercials. Later still, that talented director Jonathan Miller was able to toss scenery, costumes and tradition into the Thames and present fresh and amusing realisations of the increasingly dated operettas.

It would have been inconceivable in those Twickenham productions. Such distancing from the composer's and the librettist's original intentions would have bewildered the cast and the audience. It's safe to assume that both were supporters of the traditional middle-brow values underlying Gilbert's satires. The higher education of women was not commonplace in the thirties, so *Princess Ida* still seemed to embody a truth: women should not emulate their betters – Oxbridge men – but do the right thing by finding a mate and nesting. In *Patience* there was the chance to poke fun at Twickenham's few arty folk: those drones who did not join the commuter trains and scuttle with the worker bees towards some City hive. And there was an awareness of the original satire in that script. What else could explain the twitch of my aunt Dorothy's mouth as she outlined the plot of *Patience* to me? The shadow of Oscar Wilde and the fin de siècle decadents lingered: a preoccupation with homosexuality runs like a leitmotif just under the surface of the British mind.

It was not until I was about nine that I learned of the party on stage after the Saturday-night performance. When the last of the bouquets had been handed up and counted to make sure no bit-part player received more than the leading lady, another interesting ritual began.

The cast executed an abridged parody of their own show: the highlights, but with a difference. The private mock version was a fascinating exercise in cross-dressing. Was it local housewives playing butch Tower yeomen who enjoyed it most, or career-conscious insurance agents who could relax in a bustle and bonnet rather than in a soccer shirt? And what about the lonely ones – those who would spend that and every night without a partner? Did they watch for tell-tale signs of a shy interest among other members of the company who were, like them, still unmarried at thirty?

Every year after my fifth birthday I could reckon on attending Monday night's dress rehearsal with my grandmother. I'd go to her house when school was over. After a snack tea we'd set off, as though for a picnic, with a Thermos of coffee and a mound of sandwiches wrapped in a clean glass-cloth. My uncle and aunt would already be at the hall. It was, for me, an outing that I'd anticipated for weeks. A fresh pageant of sound and colour was about to open for me. There was the bonus, too, that I'd be able to stay up later than my usual bed-time although, as so often, my eyelids would begin to droop around half past ten. Some time after midnight my grandmother would waken me. The long rehearsal was over. As I said goodnight to Dorothy and Tom I could see from their eyes that they'd rather have been asleep, too.

Dress rehearsals were also what we'd now call a photo opportunity. There'd be someone with a camera on a tripod. He was the photographer from our local paper, sometimes referred to as *The Richmond and Twick* or, more informally, the Dimbleby rag since it was owned by the media family who then lived by Richmond Green.

The actual taking of those group photographs I found thrilling but slightly scaring. I was used to nothing more startling than fireworks on the fifth of November. The explosion of that magnesium flash suggested something of the horrors of Cousin Walter's collection of Western Front photographs.

One year – I can't be more precise – Dorothy had her first small part in one of the shows. No doubt the local photographer thought it worth recording a solo shot of her. There was always a ready sale for such stills among the cast whether a print found its way into the paper or not. Had the man been the only photographer at that dress rehearsal all would have been well.

It so happened that Tom had a contact in one of the three London evening papers. The whole cast was flattered. It was possible that home-going commuters from Uxbridge to Epping would be reading about them – even glancing at photographs of them in costume – the following day. It was natural, if unfortunate, for Tom to introduce his reporter pal and the Fleet Street photographer to Dorothy. Ready to oblige a mate with whom he'd often shared a beer-and-pie lunch, the reporter took the hint and, back in his office next morning, made his selection of suitable photographs and persuaded his sub-editor to use them.

Next evening – opening night – I went again with my grandmother to see the show. We made first for the stairs that led to the ladies' dressing-room with the refreshments for Dorothy and Tom. My aunt sat outside the room on the stone stairs weeping noisily and refusing to be comforted. There was no way that she was going to return to that dressing-room.

At best the chorus ladies were being cool to her. Most of them, as they adjusted their mob-caps, were being downright bitchy. Lying by Dorothy's feet was a copy of the London *Star*. The column inches given to Twickenham's production were generous enough. There could be no objection to that for everyone was forecasting a busy box office throughout the week. It was the two photographs that had caused the uproar. One was of the whole chorus in an ensemble with Dorothy well to the fore. The other was a shot of her dance solo.

Somehow the tensions must have been resolved for Dorothy certainly danced that night. Whether she changed into her costume on the stairs is another matter.

It was soon acknowledged that Dorothy and Tom were the show-biz branch of the family. The rest of us were rounded up for a family block-booking on the Saturday night. The rest of us included all the relatives from Portsmouth and Leicester. And Aunt Marge, of course. Who could have stopped her?

There were productions when my father's talents as a baritone were enlisted. He rightly insisted that there could be no question of his attending rehearsals during the autumn months. Money was short and work came first. So he usually joined the ever-lean male chorus very late in the rehearsal schedule. He'd a quick ear for a melody; it was the words that he could never memorise. I still see him now just as clearly as I first did, singing with uncharacteristic gusto and bonhomie in the second row. It was a long time before I realised that he was usually doing no more that vocalising a hearty la la or ah ah. For one whole ecstatic week there was the chance that I might take part in a production. From time to time there were such opportunities for a small boy: page to the Lord High Executioner or train-bearer to the Duchess of Plaza Toro. Dorothy cautioned me that I should not set my hopes too high. The musical director's son, already cast as one of Queen Elizabeth's attendants, had mumps. It seemed possible he'd not recover sufficiently to play his walk-on part. Of course he did. I sat at the end of the front row on opening night. The fury with which I stared at him was mitigated only by the promise of Dorothy's compensatory treat: a whole day, with as many ice cream cornets as I could devour, at Chessington Zoo.

TO THE DOLLS' HOUSES

that's how I thought of my occasional trips to Aunt Gladys's
various homes. I'm not suggesting that she lived with my
uncle Leonard in bijou residences. On the contrary. The
houses were much grander than any of those in which other
members of my father's family lived. Like Uncle William's
villas, they charted a progressive affluence. Unlike his, they'd
not been acquired through years of tough work and hard
bargaining. Well, not in the usual sense. I associate Aunt
Gladys, her lifestyle and her homes with leisure: opportunity
that allowed her to indulge her fantasies in clothes, provincial
snobberies and child-substitutes: other people's daughters or,
more usually, dolls.

According to family gossip, Aunt Gladys's and Uncle Leonard's lack of children was a matter of common consent. It
was left at that. Certainly it was their private business but the
ostensible reasons they gave never seemed to me, even as a
child, to add up in any convincing way. The adults around
me may also have had their own thoughts but on this, as on
almost everything concerning personal relationships or social
questions, there was little open speculation and no reasoned
debate.

So, on what did I base my private puzzlement?

One afternoon when I was seven, or maybe eight, I sat
with Gladys in a spare bedroom in her Leicester house as
she turned out old cardboard boxes and a couple of dusty
travelling cases. She knelt on a rug with a studio portrait in
one hand. I guessed that's what it was though, at first, she held
the back of the ash-grey mount towards me.

–Your uncle doesn't care for sexuality intercourse.

Uncertain what this meant, and feeling that her phrasing

100

sounded odd, I said nothing. She then turned the photograph so that I could see it. I can't pretend to recall more than the blurred sepia image of a young woman's shingled head, angled slightly to the left.

Gladys sighed.

–That's Kitty Thompson. Now, if your uncle had married her instead of me, you'd have had cousins to play with this afternoon.

I don't know what my immediate reaction was, if any. That night, before I slept, I compared my aunt with barren women in the Bible and was sorry: less for her than for the circumstances that denied me more cousins. A few years later I began to wonder whether it was a question of my aunt's infertility. Could it be that my uncle had no physical interest in her? It wasn't possible to say whether his interest in Kitty might have been keener. He'd married Gladys. That led on to another question: was his sex-drive zilch? I could have accepted this, still could, were it not for an odd phrase here and a prolonged glance there over the years. These were directed not at other women but at a robustly handsome young sportsman to whom he was distantly related, at a boxer stripped to his shorts in a fairground booth and, later, at fellow sixth-formers who might be with me when I happened to cycle over to see him.

Whatever my uncle's private frustrations and regrets, he was good company: more welcome at family gatherings than Gladys who was, at best, tolerated. We were not clannish – the phrase *blood's thicker than water* – was hers not ours, yet she was never finally accepted. Her attempts to patronise and her increasing pretentiousness were resented. As a reprisal, the other women in the family took advantage of her childlessness to patronise her behind her back:

–Too selfish, my dear, to cope with children. They'd leave her no time for all that dress-making and dolling herself up, now would they?

–Well, she's made her choice and she'll have to live with it. You can't have kids and run a show-house, can you?

No cousins for me; no children for Gladys. Only dolls. Each room in all of her successive homes housed at least one. They were, almost without exception, girls. There were Spanish señoritas and Dutch meisjies. As the year waned towards

Christmas present season, one could count on three Nell Gwynnes. Alexander Korda's film had touched something deep in Gladys. And one never needed to search far for an Elizabeth Tudor doll.

I do begin to wonder about the fascination that this particular monarch seems to have held for every branch of our family. Could it really have been the influence of Madame Tussaud's waxworks alone, reinforced by popular films and historical novels? Is it too fanciful to suppose that our predominantly Protestant family should have found, in Elizabeth I, an icon as potent a reference point as the Virgin Mary?

In addition to both geographical and historical jaunts, Gladys's creative imagination strayed annually into myth and children's tales. Each autumn brought another crop of fairy dolls ready to top the Christmas trees of relatives and neighbours. The general release of Walt Disney's *Snow White* acted as a catalyst. Swathed in a fur coat she saw the film twice before busying herself with scraps of dark velvet and white satin.

However diverse their origins, Gladys's daws – as she called them in her residual Hampshire accent – were linked by one detail common to all. Each wore a crinoline. This may have assuaged some deep romantic hunger in their creator. It was a hunger that was never sated for no sooner was one outfit complete than she began another. On and on her needle flew.

This fixation on crinolines was evident in her social life, too.

When she became relatively affluent, we were all invited to her weekend house parties.

–Just remember though, all the ladies must bring long frocks. The gentlemen will need bow ties. We'll be dressing for dinner.

On the pretext of supervising the soup or the hors d'oeuvres, she'd shoo her guests upstairs to change. Gladys was always a nagging organiser. Thirty minutes or so later the guests would assemble, as instructed, in the hall. There'd be half-hearted chatter and the sipping of dry sherry. Nigh on starving, they waited for the dinner gong to be struck at eight. It was sounded by Gladys's cleaning lady who, having been pressed into service to do the rough veg., acted as factotum for the rest of the evening. As the reverberations drifted into dark corners of the bedroom corridor, Gladys would make her entrance down the stairs – in a crinoline, what else?

In her own outfits, as in those she created for her señoritas, Nell Gwynnes and Snow Whites, she'd a notable preference for basic black. Characterisation, whenever it was necessary, was provided by a few hand props: a trug of oranges for Nell Gwynne or an ornate crucifix on a gold chain for Mary Queen of Scots ready for the chop at Fotheringay.

The crucifix was no chance accessory. At emotional moments – family weddings or funerals – Gladys would fortify herself with a few gins and then recall nostalgically her Catholic upbringing. Unlike the rest of us she would have genuflected, in an over-theatrical way, to the altar at St Mary's where so many of our hatchings, matchings and dispatchings were solemnised. Later, as we gathered round my grandmother's hearth, Gladys would remind us that she'd lived in sin with my uncle for ten or fifteen or whatever the appropriate number of years. Her own marriage out of the true faith, she'd protest, had never been recognised by the cardinal. Most of us, as we listened, were bewildered or amused by this. My grandmother, Leonard's mother, was not.

Gladys Mills came of a large Hampshire family. Her father had been a successful sheep farmer to the north of Portsdown Hill along the Petersfield road. It was there, at Asherfields House, that Gladys had been brought up during the first decade of the century. Throughout World War I the Mills family did its bit by opening the doors of Asherfields to young officers on leave from the battlefields of Northern France or from the Navy.

My only inkling of what might have gone on there came from my mother's tight-lipped asides. Given that her tongue could be censorious, it's still likely that there was some basis for her assessment:

–As far as I can hear, drink seems to have flowed swift as the Thames at Windsor. And, as for those Mills girls and the young naval officers, there was none of them any better than they should be.

Any better than they should be was my mother's Edwardian code for sex outside marriage. Who can say, three quarters of a century later, how far it might have been true? I do know that I once invited Gladys – by then a widow well into her eighties

– to a house-warming party my lover and I were giving. She giggled in her sharp metallic way before replying:

–Love to come. Do I need bother to wear my knickers?

Whoever Gladys's father may have invited to those weekend gatherings at Asherfields, he'd not have included my uncle. Leonard was an ordinary infantryman in the Hampshire Regiment. The parties were for officers only. How then did he come to meet his future wife?

He came of a modest family but he did have pleasing looks: fresh colouring, black wavy hair and lively blue eyes. More than any of these, he'd a capacity for jokes and laughter: safety valves, perhaps, against the omnipresence of death and disfiguration that he lived with in the soggy trenches by the Somme.

Somehow they did meet in Portsmouth while Leonard was on leave. Through a combination of his charm and Gladys's determination he was smuggled into Asherfields. After the Armistice the courtship continued. It's not difficult to uncover what Leonard saw in her. He admitted his post-war ambitions to his family quite openly:

–I shall marry a rich girl. I shall have a car and she can have a pink carpet in the bedroom.

Gladys was potentially wealthy so he was able, through his marriage, to achieve both car and carpet more rapidly than he might have done elsewhere. To my more sober parents they seemed a feather-headed pair. My grandfather's opinion of his youngest daughter-in-law was rather different:

–Make no mistake now. Under that fluffy little head of curls there's a quick and scheming brain.

He was not mistaken.

Having married Leonard, Gladys very soon realised that through his efforts alone she'd be unlikely to enjoy those comforts that had surrounded her in childhood. He was incapable of managing their domestic economy so she set about acquiring money of her own that would allow her to indulge her fantasies.

Her heart was set on a house more imposing than that of anyone else's in their circle. It was also set on clothes. Soon enough she'd cupboard on cupboard stuffed with frocks and with dress-lengths ready to make up into more. Long before she was forty-five she'd three fur coats.

And then she was ready, through entertaining local nobodies, to buy her way into the heart of the local Conservative Party. Although bored by the theory and practice of politics, she even attended a couple of annual party conferences. The social side enticed her. She was able to indulge herself in a change of clothes and hats twice daily for a week. It was a very special moment for her, an epiphany almost, to be mistaken on the train to Blackpool for the first Lady Eden. Her fellow-travellers may have been myopic but such a confusion would have been more credible then since there was no television coverage to give us all familiarity with visiting personalities.

A social future firmly in her sights, young Gladys filed her nails, sipped a gin, and considered just how she might acquire the means. She really had very few doubts. Her father's family had the money and most of them were stumbling through their late seventies. One ancient, who was referred to as Aunt Beat, had a fair collection of jewellery dating from Regency days. When the old girl died, only one of the nine Mills siblings inherited anything from her. In fact, Gladys got the lot.

She had also two mad uncles. I may have heard their names but I have forgotten. This pair of dotty bachelor brothers, having made a fortune in the manufacture of rupture trusses that were sold in dusty shops around the Charing Cross Road, retired to Hampshire. They actually owned the village of West Harting and they settled in the manor house.

These brothers lived to a fair age in increasingly eccentric seclusion. Their butler had instructions to serve supper not at but under the dining-room table. Like all children, I found our own dining table the perfect base for my winter camp and an equally perfect hideout at all seasons where I might be forgotten by the adults though it was long past my bedtime. How could I be other than entranced by the image of two elderly gentlemen who passed all their evenings in a similar fashion? I never met them but I pictured them as a Tweedledum and Tweedledee pair. I supposed that when Gladys and Leonard came a-courting to ensure a special place in their wills, the visitors would need to sit cross-legged on the carpet before opening any conversation.

How Gladys did it, I don't know. But she did. When the two old boys drifted finally into their long Wonderland, almost all of the Mills family inherited little or nothing. Leonard did well. Gladys did better. The major benefactor was Aunt Joyce.

Though I always thought of Gladys's homes as dead and empty, I visualised them invariably as households of three: my uncle, my aunt, and her youngest sister, Joyce. Throughout my childhood she was there, cast as something between a lodger and a skivvy.

Gladys chose, for her own purposes, to present Joyce as simple. Certainly the youngest Mills girl was uncomplicated, trusting and sensitive. As for being simple, in the sense of being unable to fend for herself or being sparsely furnished in the attic, she was not. It was Gladys who tried to ensure that her sister was ill-equipped to stand on her own feet and it was Gladys who imposed on her trusting nature. For many years, as a consequence, Joyce remained an instrument in Gladys's capable and manipulative hands.

By presenting Joyce as a simpleton and a liability, Gladys played on the sympathies and cheque books of their seemingly inexhaustible supply of ailing relatives. At the first hint of a wheeze or heart-flutter, Gladys would be away to inspect the sufferer, dragging Leonard and Joyce in tow. Having been given one of Gladys's little pep-talks, which geriatric could be so lacking in compassion as to make Joyce anything other than a major beneficiary in the will? It seems hardly necessary to add that there would always be more than a little something for my childless aunt and uncle who were so prepared to devote themselves to playing surrogate parents. The ploy never failed.

Bank balances grew healthier by the year: Joyce's most of all. By day the modest heiress worked as a counter assistant at some local post office. Most of her free time was absorbed in helping Gladys either in the kitchen, or in the bathroom where they hand-washed the blankets to save money, or in the garden where there was a good half-acre to be weeded.

At other times Joyce proved her usefulness by taking the dog, Ginger, for a run. Just for an hour at weekends, and well away from the traffic, he was allowed off the leash. So was Joyce. One Sunday afternoon when they were all in Portsmouth, a squall blew up and Joyce sheltered on a covered bench overlooking the Solent. Within minutes she was joined by a damp but fresh-faced young sailor on leave.

The couple met again the following weekend: even had tea by the South Parade Pier. Honest Joyce felt compelled to tell Gladys that she was seeing a gentleman. The elder sister's concern was instant. Let's be charitable and say it was divided equally between Joyce's welfare and her bank balance.

There was no immediate discouragement. Far from it. Quick to exploit the romantic possibilities, Gladys twittered to any one who'd listen:

–There's a lot of work involved. Joyce is an heiress so she'll have to have at least three bridesmaids. All those frocks to be made. I'm not so sure she shouldn't have seven, then I could run up a rainbow set. There's a lot to be done. . .

As Gladys's eyes gleamed at the thought of perhaps seven over-sized dolls, or maybe seven child surrogates, Joyce and her intended were doing little more than holding hands while strolling across Southsea Common.

Her sister's more manipulative hands were restless. It was peace-time. There was no need for a whirlwind courtship and the bridesmaids' frocks were a long-term project. Extra shopping trips were far more pressing. On day ticket after day ticket Joyce was taken to Kensington, Knightsbridge or Oxford Street for tours of the department stores. There was a whole trousseau to be bought and more than one bottom drawer to be lined. Bed-linen and table-wear, kitchen gadgets and dress-lengths were parcelled up. Gladys, with a more experienced eye for colour and design, usually had the final say. There were evenings when books of fashion designs were spread over the carpet and Joyce was invited to choose housecoats, afternoon frocks and a full-length creation or two for evenings out. Joyce demurred but Gladys reminded her that she was a young woman of substance. There was a bit of a fight over the need for a fur coat but Gladys won. The treks to Harrods, Maples, the Army and Navy store and Debenhams went on for months.

And then my uncle was coaxed into playing his part. Not a natural father himself, he could be guided in his role as protector of an unsophisticated virgin only by memories of how these things were done during his Victorian boyhood.

The fresh-faced sailor had to be brought home for Sunday tea and family approval.

How the meal went I can't tell but I can make a shrewd guess as to what might have been set on the lace tablecloth. Tea would have been poured from Gladys's real silver pot: something else she'd won from a deceased aunt. As to food, Gladys was never very imaginative. There would have been ham sandwiches, bread and butter and shop-bought red jam. Nor was she a good hand with a sponge cake. So there would have been what she called seedy cake – a heavy dough, nauseously loaded with caraway seeds – and lardy cake: a greasy Hampshire speciality made with lard rather than butter. These two delicacies were her own favourites and others learned to like them or go without.

An interview with my uncle followed. It's likely that he would have been sitting in the swivel chair that stood by his writing bureau. The only option open to the sailor would have been one or other of a pair of hideous but intricately carved ebony chairs inherited from the dotty uncles at Harting.

No one ever really discovered in which way or ways the sailor failed to satisfy Leonard as to his suitability during that private session. No doubt it was Joyce's future comfort and peace of mind that was uppermost in my uncle's mind.

The sailor left and was seldom referred to again. Joyce was saddened but not heartbroken. Gladys welcomed a return to the status quo ante:

–Well, I think I should say it, Joyce. The whole business has been a blessing in disguise. At least you know where you are with us, my dear. You could never have been sure where you were with a sailor. They've someone or other in every port, often enough. In any case, you've no experience of bedrooms and all that. Some men can be beasts, let me tell you.

After a decent interval – fifteen days or so – Gladys raised the question of the trousseau and the household goods for a home that was not to be. A whole bedroom was stocked with the detritus of Joyce's affair. What was to be done? Joyce sighed as she wrung out a blanket and told Gladys to take the lot. Gladys sniffed in an understanding way:

–If you think it's for the best, my dear, then I will. Of course I'll pay. . .

–I wouldn't take a penny for it, Gladys. . .

–But, Joyce, it's a lot of money. . .

–I've enough in the bank to buy half a dozen bungalows anytime, Gladys. That'll do me. You take it.

She did. So, among other things, she'd a fourth fur coat. Joyce was happy to go on warming Leonard's slippers at the fireside again while his wife got back to entertaining. By this time she was giving what she called fork lunches to the wives of councillors and aldermen on a regular basis. She'd even collected a mayor: a socialist but, nevertheless, a mayor.

On less social afternoons, when the last of Joyce's dress-lengths had been turned into a tea-gown, Gladys would set off to the shops alone. She was, in every way, a tireless bargain-hunter.

Her Christmas shopping began during the January sales. Slightly damaged goods never deterred her if the price was right. One Christmas my mother was given a clothes brush with a glaringly obvious ink stain along the handle. Even as it was being unwrapped, Gladys was pointing out not only the brand name but the royal By Appointment crest. This was more important than any stain which would not, she remarked pragmatically, hinder the brushing. It was strange that brushes were always curiously dominant in Gladys's gift lists: We got them all: brushes for our hair, our shoes, our clothes and our furniture. Sometimes we got them two years in succession. As a child I never considered whether her obsession with brushes served some deep need to remove life's excrements. But she was the only person I knew who'd run to the kitchen between courses at lunch to fetch a mini brush and dustpan. Bread-crumbs had to be removed from the cloth almost as quickly as the empty soup plates. The spilling of a drop of cream was, for Gladys, a major catastrophe.

Her snobbery was obvious at a glance. There was no one else in the family who left the price tag on Christmas presents on purpose. No one, other than Gladys, slipped a dime store gift into a Harrods bag.

How did my uncle cope with her on a day-to-day basis? I was quite young when I began to notice the regularity of his migraines and stomach upsets. Having driven home from work, he'd park the car and make immediately for his room to lie down for an hour or so. I noted his need to spend many evenings after supper preparing work for the following day. There always seemed a lot to be done before he set off again to the farthest suburbs and residual villages to sell Lever Brothers' products.

Some nights, awake in a small bedroom over the street door, I'd hear him set off on a midnight outing with the dog, first to the post box at the corner and then on towards the nearby common or heath. His cordon of solitude must have been a necessary defence against Gladys's interminable nagging and banalities.

My first exposure to my aunt in full spate came when I was eight years old. Leonard and Gladys had been staying with my grandmother in London. It was late August, so I guess we'd been on a family outing to the Bank Holiday Fair at Richmond's Old Deer Park on the Monday morning and then on to another at Hampton Court Green in the afternoon.

That August I'd been promised a holiday treat. On the Tuesday, when my aunt and uncle drove back to Leicester, they'd be taking me with them for fifteen whole days.

Today it's easy to forget that Leicester, only a hundred English miles from London, was a four-hour journey by steam train and rather more by roads that took in the old market towns of the Midlands.

After an early lunch we set off. Gladys could drive but she preferred to navigate. I sat in the back with old Mr Mills, her father. He'd long since sold Asherfields for £32,000 which, if one adds a nought and then trebles it, gives some idea of the 1992 price. A decade of hard drinking with his cronies had followed. Gladys had told us all that he'd spent the lot. Although he'd not yet been reduced to sweeping the streets of Portsmouth, the old gentleman who sat next to me was far from affluent: glad to accept pocket money from his daughter and cigarettes from his son-in-law.

As we drove north through the rain, Gladys's commentary and her advice continued almost without interruption. It's not our picnic in the car or anything of the landscape that comes to mind now. Just that twittering voice:

–Do be careful, Len. Watch out for that man in front. He's weaving all over the road. No, he's not waving you on, Len.

Do drive carefully. The man's drunk. If we go into the back of him, you'll be blamed. That's the law. . .
–All right, my dear. I'm being careful. How far's Rugby?
–Another half hour yet. Do slow down, Len. You're doing over thirty. I do wish you'd listen. They always have police traps along this stretch. . .
–Yes, my dear. . .
–Watch out for this next bend, Len. You see all those skid marks across the tarmac? I'm sure this is where the Smiths had their accident. Don't you think we ought to put the lights on? The rain's getting much heavier. . .
–Very well, my dear.
And so on, and on, and on until we reached their semi-detached villa near Leicester's De Montfort Park.
That must have been a hot summer for I remember trudging with my aunt from the house along what seemed an endless main road until we came to a distant bus stop beyond some dusty roundabout. We'd passed two much nearer stops but, having walked half-way into the city, Gladys had saved a penny or so on the fare to the market. It all seemed very odd when compared with the patronising phrase she used to others in the family:
–Well, of course, you have to realise our social positions are very different. A pound to you is a penny to me, when all's said and done.
Late in the afternoon, back from the market, I'd loll with a book in a hammock on the lawn. Above me, in a spare bed-room, Gladys's electric sewing machine would be whirring away as she knocked up yet another doll's frock. This, I knew, would continue until five minutes before my uncle was expected home for his evening meal.
Except for the Sunday roast, Gladys and Leonard appeared to exist on cold meat – usually a nice bit of ham – accompanied by a dollop of hot mashed potato and some shop-bought pickles. This would be followed by what Gladys called strewed fruit and a bit of pink. The bit of pink was, so she alleged, a favourite of my uncle's. Maybe so. Perhaps it reminded him of that pink bedroom carpet on which he'd set his sights as a young man. Perhaps he ate it, five nights out of seven, for a quiet life. Made by others, the bit of pink would have been a strawberry-flavoured

111

blancmange. Gladys concocted it with two thirds water and one third milk to save money. The result was a mound of pink half-solidified cement. It did, of course, leave more cash for a bottle of gin.

None of Gladys's close friends in Leicester had children. I couldn't talk to Ginger, the dog. After fifteen days I was more ready than I expected to be to go home with my parents when they came to collect me.

On that journey I could still hear my aunt's twittering voice with its empty chatter and its ever more numerous malapropisms. One appalling gaffe sums her up. Of an acquaintance she said:

–A most unfortunate woman. Most unfortunate. Two children, you know: one of them's plastic; the other's a mongrel.

TO HOSPITALS AND CLINICS

were rare, for my immediate family was a comparatively healthy one. Reactions to our minor ailments varied, depending on whether they were voiced by my father's or my mother's relatives. There was my father's sister-in-law, Gladys, whose obsessive quest for intimations of cancer I'll mention elsewhere. Should my parents be indisposed – even slightly – she'd scan their features for any loss of weight or characteristic yellowing at the temples. These, in conjunction, were infallible omens. Or so she said.

On my mother's side, the only contender for the Cassandra role was her sister, Florrie, who enjoyed minor afflictions in others and suffered them herself in a semi-professional way.

Quite early in life I realised that when Aunt Florrie visited, she was loaded not only with carrier bags of groceries purchased at cost through her son, Walter. She'd brought less tangible offerings. No sooner had she sunk into a comfortable chair and stirred her mid-afternoon cup of tea than she'd launch into a shopping list of recent afflictions. She expected no interruptions for the next hour, other than the reassurance of a sympathetic sigh. Should my grandmother – or anybody else – drop by unexpectedly, Aunt Florrie would grow silent, tight-lipped and baleful-eyed. She'd been thwarted and she showed it.

In general, however, my mother's family accepted and worked through the severest of head colds, as they did through bouts of that rheumatism or arthritis to which those of us who live in the Lower Thames valley are subject. If they did succumb finally to seasonal 'flu or whatever, they were down and out for some time. Having taken to their beds they seldom emerged within a fortnight.

By contrast, my father's folk would keel over more frequently, more easily, and rather more theatrically. Teeth chattered publicly and could be stilled only by the production of a medicinal brandy bottle. There'd be much gasping for breath and cracking of the voice. My mother, rather wickedly, would do private impersonations of all this. While preparing a meal, she'd pause and liken her in-laws' behaviour to deathbed performances in films that had impressed her. Her Charles II routine was much influenced by that of Sir Cedric Hardwicke:

–Don't let poor Nellie starve.

Or, looking pathetic but noble, she'd quote a phrase from one of Mrs Henry Wood's novels:

–Oh, the hectic flush on the damask cheek. . .

I'm sure I encouraged all this by guessing the response to my artful questions about aunt or uncle so-and-so's health. Almost before I went to school I was cautioned never to allow Gladys to visit my mother in bed unless she first removed what was referred to as the Abandon Hope hat. This was kept in reserve for trips she made to comfort those *in extremis*. Though my mother died of exhaustion in her ninetieth year, she never lost her horror of that hat which, she swore, could only portend terminal cancer.

However satirical her humour at what she thought of as the posturing of her in-laws, my mother was not a callous person. While dismissing most of the Robins family as a troup of amateur actors, she was genuinely sympathetic when my father faced one of his bouts of recurring malaria. This he'd contracted when my parents lived in Calcutta for the seven years that followed World War I. It afflicted him until old age and there was little the poor man could do but take to his bed and sweat it out. Quinine tablets and endless drinks of grapefruit juice helped but the fever still took its course and I saw little of him for a week.

Although unpredictable, these attacks were infrequent. More usually, my father – in common with his family – took to his room at the onset of any of the seasonal maladies. There he'd stay for a day and a half seemingly at death's door. Then – invariably – we'd hear movement overhead, and knew that he'd be with us shortly: shaved, dressed in clean collar and plain tie, an empty tea cup in his hand and a brisk question on his lips.

–Turned out not a bad afternoon at all, hasn't it? Who's for a run to Hampton Court? We could have a spot of tea in Richmond Park, if you like.

A very different recuperation from my mother's. When she finally gave in, she'd languish for weeks. In this I might well take after her. Whether it was laryngitis or quinsy, a streaming head cold or one that had gone to her chest, she felt dreadful and she looked it. Often, during the winter months, I'd tiptoe into her room as she was removing her head from a towel, having just finished inhaling vapour from a basin of the dreaded Friar's Balsam. Her hair dank and matted, the darkness of her eyes emphasised by rings of sleeplessness, she'd look at me in silence for a moment.

–Do I look terrible?

–. . . Well. . .

–Don't pretend. I do and you know it. I look like the Queen of Spain with TB. . .

Which particular Spanish consort she had in mind I was never told. One, maybe, who, like my mother, was not particularly photogenic anyway.

Almost as a ritual, incorporating a fault for which he expected to be criticised, my father would add to her discomfort. Returning from work, he'd put the kettle on the kitchen stove and then, while the water boiled, make upstairs with a gift of some flowers or a few marons glacés. All fine, so far. He was, however, a Robins. His entry to the sickroom was eager. At the door, bright of eye, he'd pause.

–Feeling better today? Must say you're looking much perkier . . .

–If you say that again, my dear, I shall scream. You'll know soon enough when I'm better. I'll be up and cooking supper instead of leaving you to fend for yourself.

We all knew – I best of all – my father's unvarying diet whenever my mother was ill or absent for any reason. There'd be boiled eggs, bread and butter, a pot of tea, stewed fruit with custard, and a wedge of sponge cake that my mother would have knocked up, either before going out for the evening or, if ill, while crawling around the kitchen in her dressing-gown. Only once did she leave us for more than a couple of nights.

It was a September evening when I found my father at work on some mysterious contraption in his large shed by our cooking-apple tree. He was painting an iron framework which I'd noticed vaguely the past couple of weekends. The thing was X-shaped at either end and had a metallic strut connecting the two crossing points. I guess I must have asked what it was since it resembled neither the sets of household shelves he often constructed nor the supporting frames he knocked up for those radio sets he was constantly repairing (unpaid) for relatives and neighbours.

My father's reply was terse.

–You're going to have a baby brother. Might be a sister, come to think of it. Whatever it is, it's a secret so don't go saying anything to anyone.

I didn't. So it was quite surprising to learn from other people, while staying at my grandmother's a few weeks later, that I did indeed have a baby brother.

My mother remained in the West Middlesex Hospital at Isleworth for thirteen weeks. The birth itself had not been complicated but there were ensuing disorders for my mother whose strength had been much depleted since she was, by then, forty-four years old.

And I stayed on and on at my grandmother's where supper wasn't always boiled eggs. There were books everywhere, cats and kittens on and under every staircase, exciting steam engines and cardboard theatres that dated from my father's childhood, and my grandmother's tales of her younger days. There were evenings when, curled in one corner of a not particularly comfortable Victorian couch, I could listen to Aunt Dorothy, Uncle Tom, and their friends rehearsing choruses from a forthcoming production of *Patience*.

At last, all these diversions palled. Not even the chance to stand with my grandmother selling paper, or linen, flowers or flags for charity could hold my interest. I wanted my mother. Relatives who called, even neighbours we met at the shops, said how much better she was beginning to look. They'd been to see her: why couldn't I?

No doubt I voiced this question as bluntly to my grandmother and aunt. One foggy afternoon in January they concocted a plan that they felt might work. It was not without theatricality.

I was to be smuggled into the hospital ward that very evening in drag.

Within minutes I was kitted out in a short jigger coat that belonged to my aunt. This I wore over one of my grandmother's high-necked blouses that had been trimmed with an enormous bow. The ensemble was topped up with an unseasonable Leghorn straw hat. Since the crown slipped to the tip of my nose, Dorothy readily saw the need for some modification.

–Wait a tick. Don't move an inch. I've just the very thing upstairs.

The very thing was a curly ginger wig that someone – my aunt or maybe my uncle – was to wear at some point in *Patience*. It seemed to do the trick. A pair of my grandmother's shoes, however, proved equally unsuccessful. Even when worn over my own they slithered uncontrollably. Since the jigger coat touched my ankles we agreed that I should retain my own grey slippers with their rabbits' ears and black button eyes.

At precisely twenty minutes to six my aunt ran in from keeping watch at the front gate.

–He's just turned the corner. Out you go and try it on him. Remember not to say too much.

Off I set, coat flapping at my heels, and wielding an umbrella much as a shepherd would his crook. In the shadows between the street lamps I came face to thighs with my uncle on his way home from an office at Victoria Station. I did my best to mutter deeply into my chest.

–Good evening.

Tom paused, a little astonished. Then he laughed, picked me up, and carried me back indoors. The conspirators hadn't intended to dash my hopes cruelly, so I didn't weep although I realised the trip was off. To compensate for my disappointment, my grandmother drew a chart and promised to pay me a penny for every day that my mother's discharge from hospital exceeded the fifteen marked on it.

Even then, during that seemingly endless winter, I knew what the inside of a hospital was like. I already associated it with a disinfectant smell and a warm sickly stench that would probably have caused me to keel over had the little old lady ruse ever succeeded.

Among hundreds of five-year-olds, I was of a generation on

whom the medical profession focused one of its occasional and obsessive fads. It was undoubtedly the schools' Medical Officer, as he toured the borough on one of his annual inspections, who diagnosed my need for a tonsillectomy. I knew nothing of the consequences until my mother packed a small case early one morning and we went by bus to Richmond Hospital. Even this seemed no special event for I was, even then, inured to a round of visits to clinics, dentists and opticians.

We lined the holly-green walls in a low, alternating frieze: parent, child, parent, child, sitting in silence on old Windsor chairs. The sexes of both children and parents alternated too, though less regularly. Mums predominated. One factor linked the children: we were all five years old. Ergo, we were of the tonsillectomy generation.

At roughly ten-minute intervals a white-clad assistant popped in from the corridor and called a couple more names. Two more tots disappeared.

–Where are they going? Why don't they come back?

–They're off to have their throats made better. You will be soon. Then you'll not have so many bad colds next winter.

I accepted this without fear, just as I accepted the bit of dressing up to which we infants were subjected. Having changed into my pyjamas, I had a hospital-issue scarlet dressing-gown slipped on me, back to front, and tied behind me at the waist. There seemed to be no reason for some of my contemporaries to start howling at this and my mother wisely offered no explanation other than a shrug. Only days later, recuperating at home, did I suspect that the scarlet dressing-gowns had been chosen on the same principle as guardsmen's tunics: the blood wouldn't show.

When my name was called I was led to another large and sparsely furnished room. Two outsize chairs, not dissimilar from those I'd seen and dreaded at various dentists' surgeries, were centrally placed. I clambered into one and sat facing a wall that consisted mainly of windows giving onto a misty morning with bare plane trees. The infant who'd accompanied me was in a similar chair to my right. Like him, I was in the care of a nurse who settled me back, lifted my chin, and fastened a rubber bib round my throat.

An implement, shaped like a gigantic metal nutcracker, was

inserted between my teeth to keep them open. This steel ball had protruberances which reminded me of the weapons carried by all genuine ogres in my comics. While I was thinking of this comparison, the nurse instructed me to breathe through a mask that she held over my nose. This was attached by tubing to a bag that resembled the inner bladder of a football. There was just about time to note that it was, in colour, a sad and rain-washed yellow.

My last sensation, as I lost consciousness, was of the back of the chair falling away behind me. This induced panic but it was too late to struggle. I felt I had been lured into a trick chair such as that owned by Sweeney Todd, the demon barber of Fleet Street. My uncle Tom had told me that story and – for a fleeting millisecond – I feared the worst. Hadn't Sweeney's victims tumbled down a chute only to reappear – bit by bit – as an ingredient in one of Mrs Lovatt's celebrated mutton pies? Was this to be my inescapable fate, with my own mother a consenting party?

Tonsils apart, I was still in one piece when I regained consciousness in yet another great cavern of a room where thin January sunlight filtered through high windows at the far end. I was lying on a mattress covered with striped ticking. On either side of me, and across an aisle along which white figures passed, were more mattresses like mine, all placed directly on a stone floor. On each mattress there was a five-year-old. We were probably three dozen in all, or a morning's work, measured by surgical yardsticks. Yet there was little weeping for I guess we must all have been too doped still from the chloroform to register discomfort.

It was, by then, late morning. Directly I was observed to be conscious, a nurse brought me a sip of water and wiped my mouth. The bib and the scarlet dressing-gown were still in place. I lost interest and drifted into a doze. This pattern continued until a large old-fashioned wall clock almost opposite me showed it to be four o'clock.

Possibly I'd been roused by new activity. Figures not in uniform were moving slowly along the aisle. Parents had arrived. Silently, they would point to one or other of my neighbours. A nod from the nurse, the small patient was gathered up and carried away, and a ward orderly brought up the rear with the relevant attaché case or carrier bag. All

119

this happened in silence or – at most – with a whispered exchange. Quite suddenly, I heard the most heart-rending wail from a far corner. One little boy, it transpired, needed overnight observation.

The wailing was still a lusty fortissimo when my own mother arrived and picked me out rather as one might select a weekend joint from the butcher's rack. With my school raincoat substituted for the dressing-gown, I was led away to be taken home once more, this time in a taxi. There was no post-surgical hanging around for ordinary folk in those pre-Health Service years.

For ten days I convalesced. Our doctor called and prescribed thrice-daily glasses of port wine, with sugar added if necessary. It most certainly was since the taste of port was repulsive to me as a child. Far more palatable was a diet of all the ice cream I could swallow. Bliss. No sooner had the cornet and wafer seller's bell sounded at the street corner than my mother would be off with a small pudding basin to collect another dollop of locally-made vanilla ice. After a day or so I pleaded for some variation: coffee perhaps, or chocolate. These hadn't been mentioned by the doctor so my mother was dubious. I'd have swallowed even her favourite (but not mine) strawberry. Vanilla it remained. To this day I never choose vanilla ice in a restaurant nor do I make it for guests.

I was a child quite content in a world of his own devising. For those keen on glib explanations it would be easy to point to the arrival of my brother Richard and link this with parental neglect of me and then scurry on, searching for signs of muted sibling rivalry. Unfortunately the facts don't square with any such theories. My sense of apartness predated my brother's birth by more than three years. It should be evident that I was never subject to parental or even grandparental neglect. It's possible the absence of blood contemporaries might, in part, have accounted for my contented solitude. Of far more impact on me was a development that precluded my ever becoming an enthusiastic participant in ball games – especially team games – of almost any kind.

One evening, lying in bed and waiting for my mother to come and turn the light out, I practised my new game. It was time, I felt, to confide in her my proficiency at what had been a private skill. She was considerably disturbed when I announced that I could see not only two light bulbs above me but, with a bit of an effort, two teddy bears set at the end of my cot bed as well.

Why was she so horrified? Why did she insist that I stop my game instantly? No explanation was given, just an instruction. Only gradually, through comments overheard, did I gather that I'd developed (undeveloped might be better) a lazy muscle in my left eye. In short, I'd a squint.

That this was far from the asset I'd supposed it to be I learned through the firm disclaimers on either side of the family that such a defect could have been inherited from them. There was even an oblique suggestion that, had my mother read to me more, rather than teaching me early to follow for myself *The Adventures of Rupert Bear* in *The Daily Express* no such catastrophe need have occurred.

Some evidence that there was a family weakness emerged many years later. Long after my grandmother's death, we were rummaging through a bag of faded photographs. There was a studio portrait no one had seen before. My grandmother Robins, hatless and in a bustled dress, was posed against some potted palms. Her head was turned slightly to one side. Presupposing the camera had not been faulty, she'd had a very discernible squint during her late teens. There were no earlier photographs of her but plenty that dated from her early twenties. The squint had obviously rectified itself for opthalmic surgery was not at its peak in Victoria's reign. Even had it been, the cost would have been beyond the purse of an ordinary Portsmouth family.

Nor does the evidence end there. Having skipped a generation to emerge in me, the lazy muscle skipped again, by-passing my niece, only to become apparent in her eldest child.

But what was to be done about me? That question was probed gently by every visiting relative and family friend. Within weeks I was fitted for glasses. This curtailed the questioning. In private I wore a black eye-patch without protest for it came in handy when playing pirates with our cat. That was not the purpose for which it had been bought. Each evening, after we had eaten, I was lifted onto the kitchen table and trained to look this way and that, following my father's hand in which he held a toffee. These exercises were deemed to coax the reluctant muscle. They did no such thing but I became very dependent on the extra source of toffees.

At six-monthly intervals I was examined by the Borough Education Committee's appointed opthalmic consultant, a Mr Blair. For an image of this austere figure, picture the Munich Prime Minister, Neville Chamberlain, add a dash more colour and style, and you have Mr Blair: Homburg hat, winged collar, grizzled moustache and all.

At the end of each consultation he advised my parents to wait until I reached adolescence before considering surgery. Another knife hung over me, though at least I knew a little of the man who'd be wielding it.

Throughout those years I wore my glasses and was deterred from playing ball games. At the time I firmly believed – as did the kids in our street and in our class at school – that this was to protect my eyes from further injury. I now suspect it was, in part, to ensure that the cost of repairing or replacing my spectacles was kept to the minimum.

Yes, there were occasional taunts of *four eyes* to which, childlike, I retorted

–Four eyes can see better than two any day of the week.

When this proved ineffective, I removed my glasses and went in with fists flailing. Whatever injunctions there were in church sermons about meek acceptance and turning the other cheek were forgotten. To this day I never accept insults, though my repayment in satire may not be as instantaneous as the bloody noses I inflicted in childhood.

Non-participation in team games has had other results. Whenever I need to catch a lighter or a bunch of keys, I do so as much by listening to the sound of the approaching object as by tracking it visually. My co-ordination between hand and eye has remained minimal though, if a picture hangs askew, or a wall has been painted ineptly at the ceiling-join, my eye is truer than that of many of my friends.

Cautioned against team games, I took with delight to swimming, cycling and athletics. Training, years later, to be a teacher, I combined English with Physical Education. With all the pretentiousness of a student I invented a cover story that I wished to combine the classical aims of Greece: musica and gymnastica. What more was that than a wish to appear as macho as my contemporaries?

Adolescence lies beyond the covers of this book but, on balance, I feel the solution to the squint problem should be noted.

By my sixteenth year I knew I was leaving the Thames valley to become a teacher. No way was I going to be encumbered with glasses which, once removed, might reveal a glaring defect. There'd already been a few nights in my young life when I'd shared a bed. I'd no wish to continue a pattern of turning away to undress and then – at the risk of appearing to be of oriental extraction – peering slit-eyed in search of a light switch.

At the six-monthly check-up, I pleaded with Mr Blair to book me in to Richmond Hospital again. Would I need to sit bandaged like some shot-down R.A.F. hero waiting for that magic morning when my eyes would be unbound and, like most others, I'd see just one sun, however much I screwed up my eyes? It was a self-dramatisation that blended hope and terror.

I packed a case one July morning, prepared to spend three weeks in darkness and tried to comfort myself that it really was not so very different from having my tonsils snipped.

Mr Blair gave me yet another once-over before taking off his own glasses and starting beyond me towards Richmond Green. We'd been through the usual routine of a pencil torch held close to my eyes while I looked up, down and every which way. Mr Blair's silence seemed interminable but I didn't dare interrupt for, by all accounts, he didn't suffer patients' questions easily.

He cleared his throat at last but still didn't look at me.

–Going to be an actor, are you? Something of that sort? One of these film stars?

–No. I'm going to be a teacher.

Another pause and then he stared at me.

–Be wearing glasses by the time you're forty then, won't you?

It was now or never. I had to state my case.

–But I'm only just sixteen. I don't want to wear them now. . .

–No reason why you should. . .

–Would you want to go around with a squint?

It was said. The clerical assistant in the corner glanced up, perhaps expecting a storm. Mr Blair's glance hardened, then relaxed and he almost smiled. But only almost.

–You have a point. My boy, there's virtually nothing wrong with your eyes. If people were more patient my work would be halved. I could do a snip here and there if you insist. No guarantee that the eye wouldn't turn out the other way in another twenty years. Best to keep your glasses but wean yourself from them. I can't make you look the world in the eye. . . Now, what's this? Not going to weep on me, are you?
–Sorry. It's the tension . . . operations and all that.
–Nothing to get upset about. I do half a dozen most weeks. Blow your nose and tell them to send in the next one. You'll not see me again. Good luck with your teaching.

So that evening, not temporarily blind and motionless after all, I made for the phone booth at the corner of our street. I arranged a meeting that neither of us had expected under the willows towards Richmond Bridge. It was dusk, so I took off my glasses and lied that I'd broken them. No comment. I lied again, saying that I'd not need to visit my Portsmouth relatives for the next three weeks after all. No comment; just a smile. We moved closer. It was daunting to have my eyes inspected again but pleasurable since it was not Mr Blair who was smiling into them.

THAT ENDED IT ALL

When I opened our front door to my uncle Tom that Saturday afternoon, I noticed two odd things about him. He was wearing an overcoat I'd not seen before. True, it was a cold day and Christmas was only two weeks off but why had he discarded his usual tawny raglan tweed in favour of a much more formal black? Although it was far from new, the style of the coat struck me: it was something that I associated with undertakers, or with Uncle William Robinson when he was off on one of his jaunts to a première or a charity supper at the Dorchester.

Secondly, my uncle's face was curiously solemn. It was as though he were about to rebuke me for something I'd done – and that was not often. When he spoke, there wasn't the half-joking tone I'd come to expect of him:

–Is your Dad in?

Of course he was. We'd only just finished lunch and both my parents were at the back of the house. I'd come from the sitting room where I'd been reading a story to my brother.

–Yes, they're both in. Come on, I'll take you through.

–No, you go on back in the warm. I want a word with him alone.

Back I went and left them to it. My brother was waiting on the rug in front of our new electric fire with its imitation coals that concealed a red light-bulb and a fan that made almost realistic flames. While they spread patterns on the ceiling that damp overcast afternoon, I continued with the story of Pinnochio.

I can't say for how long but suddenly the door opened and my father stood there, his eyes red and a handkerchief held to his nose. Over his shoulder I saw my mother. She'd removed her glasses and was sobbing.

–Your grandmother's dead.

I knew what the words meant but just didn't feel they could be true. Wouldn't it be my grandmother's birthday in three days' time? Hadn't a party been arranged and all of us invited? Dead? How could she be? It was not as though she had been ill. She'd had a couple of heavy nose-bleeds some months earlier but they, so everyone had agreed, were caused through working too long without a hat on hot August afternoons in her garden.

I joined in the howling not merely because everyone else had started again. The news prompted in me a series of images, each connected with deprivation. I'd no longer meet her by chance as she walked her aged Airedale, Tigilinus and per-suade her to buy me chips. There'd be no more evenings on which, walking me home, she and I would play *Knock 'em down Ginger*, a game we both enjoyed. She or I would ring the doorbells of her respectable Conservative Party friends and then, hidden behind their garden hedges, observe bewildered glances along Twickenham's quieter avenues. Nor would I be able to dance with her again in her kitchen as she transformed a saucepan lid into a tambourine and parodied Salvation Army hymns such as:

Jesus bids us shine with a clear, pure light
Like a little candle, shining in the night;
He looks down from Heaven to see us shine:
You in your small corner and me in mine.

I wept because I was overwhelmed by the realisation that I'd never see her again. Within days she'd be no more than another corpse in one of those black coffins that had stood before me so many times as I sang at funeral services by the chancel steps.

After the first grief I realised something else. Although she would have gone, her house would still be there. Every room would echo with her voice or footsteps. I'd see her coming towards me in the garden on tranquil afternoons with sandwiches she'd knocked up from home-grown tomatoes peppered with the addition of nasturtium leaves. The daffo-dils would be coming up in a few months around her tiny lawn. She'd not be there to hack at them with her kitchen knife or to arrange great bunches of them in the sitting room.

Aunt Dorothy and Uncle Tom would still be in the house to

welcome me. I'd continue to go to their flat on the two top floors. I felt certain of that. Not that it would be the same. They'd a toddling daughter of their own and they were beginning to grow apart from my grandmother anyway. Visiting them all in that tall Victorian villa was over. Calling on my aunt and uncle would become no more special than dropping in on any of the relatives.

My mother sewed a black armband on my raincoat. It made me a temporary focus of interest in the school playground during those days before the funeral. I felt no sense of importance when telling those who enquired that my grandmother had died. The questions irritated me. They interrupted those memories of her that I re-ran constantly, rather as I re-ran short strips of film in my noisy electric cinematograph.

I'd visualise us climbing into what I called a coach and she called a charabanc to join a couple of dozen pensioners all heading for a day out at the coast. She'd always been quick to spot advertisements for a cheap day-trip to Portsmouth. Naturally, I'd have my bucket and spade since we'd make time for a couple of hours on the beach. And later, either we'd pop in to see her sister Frances in a frowsy bed-sitter off the Commercial Road or we'd take a local bus over Portsdown Hill to Horndean.

From the Red Lion pub in the square, we'd tramp away over windy north-facing slopes to the smallholding of her brother, Richard Silversmith. He was a shadowy figure: no more than a tall, wiry man with a slight stoop who joined us at the tea-table. His wife, Nell, I wouldn't have recognised in the street had I come face to face with her between visits. Summer or winter she appeared to me to be a vast ball of beige wool. Short and rotund, she swaddled herself in knitted garments. The hair that strayed from her head resembled hanks that that had been formed from a recently unravelled cardigan. My most lasting memory of their homestead was an outside earth privy that stank only a little less than some I've used more recently in Zambia or Kashmir.

There'd be no more bargain-hunting expeditions with my grandmother along the second-hand shops in Heath Road. That occurred to me as I raced through classroom tests at double speed so that I could generate more time to think of what had been. I supposed that I'd continue to lift my school cap and say *Good morning* to Old Gratton as I passed his shop. He was a firm acquaintance of my grandmother's and knew well enough she was no fool when it came to furniture.

During her widowhood she'd developed a critical eye for early Victoriana and the occasional Regency piece. In the thirties such items were still considered, often enough, to be no more than a lot of old-fashioned junk. It was quite usual for them to be cleared from homes after a death, together with broken shoes and chipped ewers and basins. She taught me, when I was very young, to distinguish between red mahogany and rosewood, yew and pine. I learned that one should always turn chairs, occasional tables and chests upside down to check their authenticity. Were there butterfly hinges? Had wooden pegs been used? Was the article only a hybrid: no more than a crafty cannibalisation of two or more pieces so dilapidated that, in themselves they were fit just for firewood?

She bought town pieces, not what she called country ware. Oak, beech and elm were not to her taste. The rosewood escritoire that she once bargained for at Old Gratton's cost half her widow's pension that week. It would sell today for a college lecturer's monthly salary.

Such images of her recurred almost endlessly throughout those mid-winter days. Even after school, when I'd usually be racing home to eat my tea before leaving to sing carols in the more affluent parts of the town, there was no escaping such memories. My mother felt it would not be right for me to go singing for money that year. It was a severe blow to my Christmas present budget and I told my mother that friends and relatives shouldn't expect too much. So each evening, too, I was free to mull over what now had to be thought of as the past rather than continuous. I visualised, without unease, that body decomposing slowly in its chilly front bedroom.

I used my unseasonable leisure to write my last will and testament. My Hornby train and model farm I left to my small brother, Richard. My books were to go to my school friend Roger, who was a great reader. My fairy cycle, which I was rapidly outgrowing, was to be given to Alec. I directed that he should sell it and enjoy the proceeds in bottles of Tizer and Cream Soda to which he was addicted. The contents of my post office savings book – all those sixpenny stamps purchased over the months – went to my mother. There was a proviso. The money was to be spent on Billy, our cat. He was always my far from willing accomplice in adventures to desert islands and through tropical jungles. My legacy was to be in the form of regular supplies of boiled whiting because I knew it was a treat to which he was very partial. The whole document, written adult-style with joined-up letters, was inscribed on the pages of a squared exercise book. I placed it in an envelope, sealed it with wax, and lodged it in the right-hand cupboard of our Dutch dresser.

It was not the omnipresence of death that prompted me to make that will. It was a new word, will, a new term in my life – and one that was much in the air during those days surrounding my grandmother's funeral. I began to understand that there could be unforeseen complications if one did not leave such a document. There were muttered allusions by my mother when my father was away at work. Doubtless both my parents had discussed the matter that bleak Saturday afternoon when the news had been broken to us but I'd not been present. Immediately before and after the funeral, however, I heard my mother deploring the absence of a will to her own relatives and friends. I myself had no idea whether my grandmother had died rich or poor. For me, relatives were divided between those who, on leaving, gave me a mere pat on the head and those who tipped me half a crown.

And then, unexpectedly, there was a fresh development to be analysed over the teacups. A whole new twist to the mystery. A will had been discovered but it had not been signed.

–Ah, but just how valid would it be in law, eh? Answer me that.

Valid: another new word. The point appeared to be that my grandmother's four children, my father being the eldest, might or might not agree to respect her unsigned wishes. If they didn't, I guessed there'd be another family row.

–Naturally we'll not contest the matter. I must say, though, that the phrasing used was really hurtful to the parties concerned.

The phrasing to which my mother objected was the specific difference my grandmother had made between her youngest son and her two elder boys. I doubt whether she'd meant it intentionally. Then, as now, people react with odd passions and vehemence when faced with sudden death. Maybe my grandmother did think more kindly of her youngest son, Leonard. Of the three, he was the one who most resembled her physically and he'd had narrow escapes in three battles during the 1914-1918 war.

There were dark hints of golden guineas that might well have been secreted under the dining-room carpet. The implication was plain. Aunt Dorothy, having been her mother's tenant, had had the leisure and opportunity to discover undreamed-of wealth. Could she have uncovered a hoard? Had she dared my uncle Tom to disclose, even by the twitch of an eyebrow, that the two of them were hiding tainted money?

True, they'd been married only four years and my uncle was still only an ordinary clerk in the continental bookings section at Victoria Station. Equally true, the two of them were ambitious. On the other hand, they were harder workers than anyone else in the family. That became ever more obvious in subsequent years. To have suggested that they were the Macbeths in modern dress was ludicrous. They were guilty only of having the misfortune to be in a house where a death had occurred. That is always more than enough for ungenerous minds.

In addition to such jewellery and furniture as she possessed, my grandmother left her leasehold house to be sold so that the sum realised could be divided equally between her four children. That distant uncle who'd once troubled my Christmas morning by ruffling my hair too tenderly was called in. He was an estate agent and valuer. The house was assessed at £200.

The four beneficiaries met in our dining room before the funeral. My aunt, as resident tenant, was offered first refusal if she wanted to buy out her brothers with a series of quarterly cheques. This was commonsensical since they already had homes of their own. But the offer must have been only a formality. The answer was known before the question was put.

Aunt Dorothy had packed two cases within hours of her mother's death. She'd moved across town to her mother-in-law's, declaring she'd never spend another night in the house. It was clear that she feared the imprint of her mother's personality would linger in the house. She was only expressing more forcefully what I myself thought at the time. For her it was no less than a conviction that neither dismissive laughter nor reason could shake: the energy liberated so suddenly by my grandmother's heart attack would not be dispelled for years. It would not have seeped only into the furniture – that could be moved elsewhere. It would have also permeated the wallpaper and the plaster beneath with such impact that she would be there: not visibly and not fancifully; inescapably.

How long did Dorothy's discussions with her brothers continue before my father indicated that he would buy the house and we'd move in? I never heard. My uncle Ted's business, his friends and his many relatives by marriage, were in Hampshire. He'd no interest in moving to Twickenham. Leonard was buying elsewhere and Gladys would have deemed the purchase of a mid-Victorian semi as a social come-down. Their grand four-bedroomed villa, recently acquired, overlooked open fields that sloped from Bushey Heath towards Watford on the skyline. It was modern, impressive and more convenient for him, as a sales rep. From his base there he could tour the just-built north-western suburbs, each with its surface level underground station, its Woolworths, Boots the Chemist and a Freeman, Hardy and Willis shoe shop. What point for him in swopping all that for a spacious but draughty house built in 1865 for the then bandmaster of the Military School of Music at Kneller Hall?

It's quite probable my mother urged my father into buying; he needed the occasional push. She was doubly right to do so. Those cheques for £2.50, sent to his three relatives each quarter day, bought bricks and mortar until, shortly after the war, the property was his. Uncle William Robinson would have made the logic of all this plain. The financial commitment amounted to little more than the 13s 6d weekly rental that was paid on our smaller terraced house. There were local rates and the ground rent to be met but my father had just been taken on staff at work. Although his job was not pensionable, there was some stability. It was the winter of 1938-39 and, at the factories, people talked endlessly of turning over to war work.

–I'm glad she didn't live to see all this.

Aunt Dorothy, in black like the rest of us, dabbed her nose. She was nodding through the window of the second car behind the hearse as she spoke. We all looked. The cortège was

131

passing Twickenham Green at the time. Although I knew the route well enough, I could see that there were changes among the bare chestnut trees and the unused cricket pitches. Preparations for war were apparent. Gangs of unemployed men had been recruited by the Council to dig deep trenches prior to the construction of concrete public air-raid shelters. Various aunts around me sighed and nodded. Aunt Dorothy, though a blood relative, was with us in the second car, having made it plain that she'd rather not sit contemplating the back of the coffin.

How many cars were there? Four certainly; more likely five. In addition to the extended family, there were one or two old dears my grandmother had befriended. Most memorable was Mrs Leverton. A funeral made little difference to her appearance for she dressed invariably in black. Minute, and walking in all weathers with an umbrella, she resembled a brittle, lacquered beetle with her string of jet beads, her widow's bonnet and her restless dark eyes set in a leather-brown face. My grandmother alleged she'd met the old dear at a church bazaar and had taken her home for a cup of tea. It may have been so. I do recall that she seemed to pop in daily whenever I stayed at my grandmother's. She was a widow nearer eighty than seventy who appeared to have been deserted by her family. Though she pretended to be penniless, she was not. I heard her often enough recounting her holidays and trips to friends in towns not on our circuit. Each place she named conjured for me landscapes that were either sad or grey: Dymchurch and Lowestoft. Some of her haunts evoked vistas sloping gently under a January sun that offered little warmth: Sydenham and Norwood and Denmark Hill.

Need it be added that Aunt Marge was at the funeral, tucked into a corner of one of the other cars? She wore a black lamb's wool coat with only the merest suspicion of heliotrope in her scarf. When someone pointed to this with a raised eyebrow she explained that heliotrope, being a variant of purple, could be worn:

–It is a shade much favoured for royal mourning.

That little interchange took place as we were gathering at lunch-time in my grandmother's house. I'd not seen it more crowded since the morning of Dorothy's wedding when I'd been a page boy.

As we waited for the hearse, most people circulated and chatted quietly in the ground-floor rooms. It was difficult to stand and balance a tea-cup in the sitting room. There was nowhere to sit. The chairs, the chaise longue, the piano and the side-tables, as well as most of the carpet, had been covered with flowers. There were wreaths and sprays from neighbours, from the local Conservative Party, from the Operatic Society and from local shopkeepers. Of course there were flowers from the immediate family as well as from one or two relatives of whom I'd never heard. From her grandchildren: my girl cousin, my brother and me, there were posies. My cousin Norman, being seventeen and about to join the Grenadier Guards, counted as an adult.

From time to time I noticed people going upstairs. At first I supposed they must be wanting to wash their faces or straighten their ties or hats. Since everybody who did so returned weeping, I soon deduced that my grandmother must still be in the house. Far from unnerving me, it only confirmed my feeling that she would never leave. I was probably thinking about this as the cars drew up outside.

–Do you want to come and see your grandmother for the last time?

I looked up at Dorothy and nodded. Of course I did. If it was to be the first dead body I was to see, it couldn't be a kindlier one. That the undertaker's men were waiting to screw down the coffin lid did not occur to me.

The coffin was set on a trestle in the large front bedroom. It was next to that double bed in which I'd so often slept when younger. My grandmother's hair was as silver as I'd supposed it would be but the curls were rather more orderly. Her head rested on a white satin pillow. I stood silently while Dorothy held my hand and cried. After a moment or so I, too, began to howl. It was astonishment and horror that moved me more than grief. My grandmother's eyes were half open and weak sunlight through the net curtains touched the glassy blue irises that had once been so full of merriment. My howling turned to screams and I dragged my aunt from the room:

–She can still see me. She can.

As much for her own peace of mind as for mine, Dorothy assured me that it just couldn't be and that, even had my terror been more than an illusion, my grandmother would never harm me. I knew all that well enough but I knew what I'd seen. Only much later did I realise that, to a small boy, those eyes were indeed half open. The adults looked down. I was level with the corpse and looked across. The lids had not been fully closed.

It really did not matter to me in which car I travelled to and from the cemetery. Nor, I suspect, did many other of the mourners give a damn about any order of precedence. Except Aunt Gladys. Always good on a death was Gladys. She'd had more experience than the rest of us. There was always one or other of her own great cluster of relatives about to succumb to some mortal disease. The incidence of cancer in the Mills family would have been the wonder of statisticians had she provided them with progress reports as regularly as she did us.

Death never caught Gladys unprepared. She'd more than one mourning outfit but the hat never varied. She was particularly proud of a black straw trimmed with osprey feathers. This was referred to generally as Gladys's Abandon Hope hat:

–If she comes round here in that damned thing next time I have 'flu, I'll turn my face to the wall like Henry II and never smile again.

It never happened, since she visited our branch of the family less than frequently. Gladys was never keen on my mother's relatives for she'd been sorely wounded by one of them. At a funeral, as it happens, long before I was born. Bearing down on my mother's second cousin, a successful lawyer from Inverness, she twittered too loudly:

–Ah, Sir Alexander, I suppose you could say we're almost related. . .

–Indeed, madam?

–Well, I'm married to Elizabeth's brother-in-law and you're a cousin of her mother's so you might say we're third cousins. . .

–*You* might, madam. We Scots don't recognise third cousins.

But that was elsewhere and at another funeral.

It was Gladys's experience of precedence that allowed her to win the slight contretemps that took place as we left the graveside in a long and muted straggle. The three brothers and their sister took the first car since there was no longer a hearse for Dorothy to face. This still left a fifth

134

and hitherto unused place. My mother demurred but Gladys insisted that as senior daughter-in-law she should take it. My mother, with uncharacteristic submissiveness, was propelled physically into the car.

I was in the second car again: this time with Gladys, my aunt Maud and my cousin Norman. Somewhere along the route to that echoing house where drinks and sandwiches had been set out, my cousin Norman broke down. He, too, had loved my grandmother:

–Isn't that funny, now. I can't say I've ever seen a man cry before.

Witless as ever, Aunt Gladys whinnied away. It didn't help Norman. If what she said was true then the Mills family must have been a pretty hard-boiled lot. While my cousin continued to blow his nose, Aunt Maud lit a cigarette and stared at the open trenches on Twickenham Green. And Gladys? She prattled on.

I didn't bother to listen. Once more, I was re-running in my mind those anecdotes my grandmother had told me so often – stories I needed to hear for I'd have to tell them to myself in future. Of her walks with my grandfather on the Isle of Wight when they'd been a courting couple. Such accounts of Sunday outings meant little to me in themselves. They came alive only when she mentioned the gaunt and stooping old man who stood alone at his garden gate watching the passers-by:

–Scruffy as a gypsy he was. His beard needed a darned good combing. As for his fingernails, my dear, you could have grown radishes in them. He'd stare right through us, looking down the lane. Your grandfather and I would joke about who he was expecting to turn up. It certainly wasn't Maud.

They had indeed seen Lord Tennyson. My own mother could recite yards of *The Lady of Shallott* as she peeled the potatoes; my father would sing *Come into the garden, Maud*, but my grandmother had seen the ancient laureate.

I had to accept that she'd not be able to describe again for me the procession and gun-carriage that had carried the body of Queen Victoria from Portsmouth Harbour to the Guildhall Square where the coffin had been put on a train at that same Town Station in which we were always met by Aunt Marge. My father had good cause to remember the Queen's funeral: he'd tumbled from a wall onto which he'd climbed for a better view of the soldiers. I don't recall that he ever mentioned it once.

–Gladys, don't be silly. Anything that was worth mentioning was set out in the will. The rest of her bits can be divided between us and what's left over can go to a jumble sale.

I heard Aunt Maud's rebuke. It jolted me back to the then and there. I resolved never to go near a jumble sale for a whole year. I'd no wish to see my grandmother's clothes or ornaments displayed on a bric-à-brac stall.

Somebody had to mention Christmas as we sat, an hour later, by the fireside in my grandmother's sitting room. Most probably it was my uncle Ted. Unspoken reproaches of tactlessness would have meant little to him when weighed against practicalities. Christmas was only ten days off. There could be no question of a family gathering. It was agreed that each branch of the family should have its own mini-Christmas with perhaps a quiet visit here and there for a cup of tea on Boxing Day.

The Christmases of childhood were over for me, though I didn't know it. Already, as they sat around the fire, the adults were distracting themselves from their sense of loss with talk of the war that was coming. I listened to their speculation. The only thing to which I could relate it was those gory photographs of the Western Front near a river called the Somme, hundreds of miles away. It did not cross my mind that war could affect Christmas or the annual patterns of family life that I'd come to expect. My relatives, with the exception of cousin Norman, could measure it against an earlier war: the losses in action, rationing and even a few haphazard air-raids.

If they guessed that there'd never be another Christmas at *The Dolphin*, or that by the time the war was over the family might well be widely dispersed, they did not say. No one could imagine how long it might last or whether even I, in a few years, might be liable for conscription.

The speculation distracted us all from dwelling too long on an irretrievable past. Soon it was time for us to separate, leaving the house empty.

I was too old by then to be carried on my father's shoulders across the Station Yard. So I walked between my parents and Norman who was staying overnight with us. We took the road that ran parallel with the railway tracks for half a mile. Then we turned away and towards the bakery where, whatever the weather, the cellar trap-doors were open so that the smell of baking bread rose in a steam under our noses.

Although I did not say so, I'd every hope that Norman and I would be sharing a room that night. The alternative would have been a make-shift bed on a couch for me.

We did share what my mother called our three-quarter bed. When the light had been switched off, it was comforting for me to have my seventeen-year-old cousin's arm round me. I snuggled against him and asked if he would be scared when the war began. He thought about it and then shrugged:

–It's all part of the job, really. When it's peace-time you wear a red uniform and help to guard the King and Queen and find the girls giving you the eye. When there's a war you wear khaki and fight. That's about it. . .

Suddenly his voice became unsteady and I could hear him gulp. I knew he was thinking of our grandmother and I began to snivel. His chin was in my hair so I could feel his face rotating in his misery.

–You'll miss her, too, won't you?

I sobbed that of course I would. When he'd helped me to blow my nose I tried to look up at him in the shadows. He pushed my head down onto his chest and hugged me tight.

Then he said something that seemed very strange:

–Why couldn't you have been a girl?

I remember laughing and saying that I wasn't and that just couldn't be helped. He laughed, too, and added that it might have helped a bit. There seemed no sense in this. Weren't we comfortable enough already, I thought, snuggled into each other on that extra-chilly night? Yet he'd roused my curiosity:

–Why do you wish I'd been a girl, Norman?

There was a pause before he replied:

–It doesn't matter. Let's sleep, eh?

So we did, and that was just as well. Had we moved from a cousinly embrace to something closer, he would have forgotten it sooner than I should have done.